Thinking Critically:
Mass Shootings

Andrea C. Nakaya

ReferencePoint
Press®

San Diego, CA

© 2015 ReferencePoint Press, Inc.
Printed in the United States

For more information, contact:
ReferencePoint Press, Inc.
PO Box 27779
San Diego, CA 92198
www.ReferencePointPress.com

Picture Credits:
Maury Aaseng, 9, 16, 22, 29, 36, 41, 47, 54, 60

LIBRARY OF CONGRESS CATALOGING IN PUBLICATION DATA

Nakaya, Andrea C., 1976-
 Thinking critically. Mass shootings/by Andrea C. Nakaya.
  pages cm. -- (Thinking critically)
 Includes bibliographical references and index.
 ISBN 978-1-60152-822-3 (hardback) -- ISBN 1-60152-822-1 (hardback)
 1. Firearms and crime--United States--Juvenile literature. 2. Violent crimes--United States--Juvenile literature. 3. Mass murder--United States--Juvenile literature. 4. Gun control--United States--Juvenile literature. I. Title.
 HV7436.N353 2016
 364.152'340973--dc23
                                                              2014040908

Contents

Foreword

"Literacy is the most basic currency of the knowledge economy we're living in today." Barack Obama (at the time a senator from Illinois) spoke these words during a 2005 speech before the American Library Association. One question raised by this statement is: What does it mean to be a literate person in the twenty-first century?

E.D. Hirsch Jr., author of *Cultural Literacy: What Every American Needs to Know*, answers the question this way: "To be culturally literate is to possess the basic information needed to thrive in the modern world. The breadth of the information is great, extending over the major domains of human activity from sports to science."

But literacy in the twenty-first century goes beyond the accumulation of knowledge gained through study and experience and expanded over time. Now more than ever literacy requires the ability to sift through and evaluate vast amounts of information and, as the authors of the Common Core State Standards state, to "demonstrate the cogent reasoning and use of evidence that is essential to both private deliberation and responsible citizenship in a democratic republic."

The Thinking Critically series challenges students to become discerning readers, to think independently, and to engage and develop their skills as critical thinkers. Through a narrative-driven, pro/con format, the series introduces students to the complex issues that dominate public discourse—topics such as gun control and violence, social networking, and medical marijuana. All chapters revolve around a single, pointed question such as Can Stronger Gun Control Measures Prevent Mass Shootings?, or Does Social Networking Benefit Society?, or Should Medical Marijuana Be Legalized? This inquiry-based approach introduces student researchers to core issues and concerns on a given topic. Each chapter includes one part that argues the affirmative and one part that argues the negative—all written by a single author. With the single-author format the predominant arguments for and against an issue can be synthesized into clear, accessible discussions supported by details and evidence including relevant facts, direct quotes, current examples, and statistical illustrations. All volumes include focus questions to guide students as they read each pro/con discussion, a list of key facts, and an annotated list of related organizations and websites for conducting further research.

The authors of the Common Core State Standards have set out the particular qualities that a literate person in the twenty-first century must have. These include the ability to think independently, establish a base of knowledge across a wide range of subjects, engage in open-minded but discerning reading and listening, know how to use and evaluate evidence, and appreciate and understand diverse perspectives. The new Thinking Critically series supports these goals by providing a solid introduction to the study of pro/con issues.

Mass Shootings

In July 2012 twenty-three-year-old Julia Vojtsek and her boyfriend, twenty-seven-year-old John Larimer, went to a Colorado movie theater for a midnight screening of the new Batman movie, *The Dark Knight Rises*. They were so excited about the movie that they arrived at the theater wearing Batman shirts, capes, and masks. Eighteen minutes into the movie, excitement turned to horror. Dressed in protective gear and armed with numerous firearms, twenty-four-year-old James Holmes opened fire on dozens of movie watchers. He killed twelve people, including Larimer, and wounded fifty-eight more. While Vojtsek survived, her life was irrevocably changed. In an interview a year later, she said she lost about 40 percent of her hearing as a result of the loud gunfire and has struggled to deal with post-traumatic stress disorder. At Holmes's trial, prosecutor Karen Pearson argued that Holmes was trying to inflict even greater damage than he did. She said he chose this location because the victims were trapped in a small space and easy to shoot. Pearson says, "He intended to kill them all."[1] Holmes pleaded not guilty by reason of insanity; his trial was slated to take place in 2015.

Over the past twenty years, research shows mass shootings have occurred almost every year in the United States—although not always with as many victims as in the Colorado movie theater shooting. And many years have seen more than one such shooting. As often as mass shootings take place, they still lead to much debate as people try to understand why these crimes occur and how they might be reduced.

Multiple Victims and Other Common Elements

There is no official definition of a mass shooting; however, most people agree that it is a single incident—not something that happens numerous times or over days or weeks—and involves multiple victims of gun violence. Most estimates of mass shootings include only those incidents in which a certain number of people die. Up until recently most researchers have used four or more deaths. In 2014, however, the Federal Bureau of Investigation (FBI) defined a mass killing as an incident in which three or more people die. Others broaden the definition to include any attack that results in multiple victims, regardless of whether they are injured or killed.

The political magazine *Mother Jones* has done extensive research on mass shootings. It gives an example of how sticking to the definition of three or more deaths can be problematic: "Was it not a 'mass shooting' in 2008, for example, when a man walked into a church in Tennessee and opened fire with a shotgun, killing two and injuring seven?"[2]

Despite disagreement over what constitutes a mass shooting, studies show that most such events have certain characteristics in common. The gender of the shooter is one common characteristic; most shooters are male. Other than that, the characteristics of shooters vary widely. In a 2013 report on mass shootings, the Congressional Research Service concluded that there is no typical profile of a shooter. The report says, "Aside from usually but not always being male, there are few other characteristics across mass murderers that would be reliable or valid for creating a general profile for individuals most likely to engage in a public mass shooting."[3] Another shared characteristic of mass shootings is time frame; most end relatively quickly. According to a 2014 FBI analysis of US shootings, of those in which the duration could be determined, 69 percent ended in five minutes or less. Research on mass shootings also shows that

> "There are few . . . characteristics across mass murderers that would be reliable or valid for creating a general profile for individuals most likely to engage in a public mass shooting."[3]
>
> —The Congressional Research Service is a public policy research organization.

many shooters use semiautomatic weapons, which can quickly fire many shots, and that they commonly obtain their weapons legally. According to *Mother Jones*, of mass shootings that have occurred since 1982, approximately half of the weapons used were semiautomatic handguns, and more than three-quarters of the weapons used were obtained legally.

Gun Laws

Gun purchases are regulated by both state and federal laws. State laws vary widely. For example, Connecticut requires a permit to purchase a gun, while Alaska does not. Federal gun laws, on the other hand, apply nationwide. Federal law requires that all businesses selling firearms must be federally licensed to do so. Licensed sellers are also required to conduct background checks on gun buyers. Certain groups of people are not allowed to purchase a gun, including convicted felons, those who have ever been committed to a mental institution, and people who have been convicted of crimes of domestic violence. However, although background checks are required by law, some people manage to avoid them by purchasing a gun from a private seller, in which case a background check is not required. Research shows that a large number of gun purchases happen this way.

Laws about carrying guns in public also vary by state. Some states have strict regulations that require gun owners to complete training and obtain a permit; however, in other states, like Arizona, residents can carry a concealed weapon in public without a permit of any kind. According to a 2012 report by the Government Accountability Office, only Illinois and the District of Columbia do not allow citizens to carry concealed handguns.

Following the 2012 shooting in Newtown, Connecticut, many lawmakers proposed new gun laws in an attempt to prevent future mass shootings. However, despite such efforts, most experts believe that in recent years gun laws in the United States have actually become less strict. For example, in 2013 news organization CNN reported that following the Newtown shooting, at least five states tightened gun laws, but more than a dozen loosened them.

Where Mass Shootings Occur

Since 1996 dozens of mass shootings (involving an active shooter who shot three or more people in a single event) have taken place in the United States. Data collected by the Stanford University Geospatial Center for its Mass Shootings in America project reveals that about 40 percent of these shootings have occurred in various school settings, and about 20 percent have taken place in business settings.

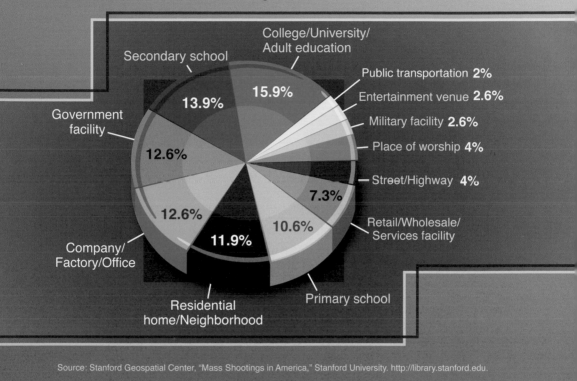

College/University/Adult education

Secondary school

Public transportation **2%**

15.9%

Entertainment venue **2.6%**

13.9%

Military facility **2.6%**

Government facility

Place of worship **4%**

12.6%

Street/Highway **4%**

7.3%

12.6%

Retail/Wholesale/Services facility

10.6%

Company/Factory/Office

11.9%

Residential home/Neighborhood

Primary school

Source: Stanford Geospatial Center, "Mass Shootings in America," Stanford University. http://library.stanford.edu.

Extent of the Threat

Because there is no official definition of what constitutes a mass shooting, there are varying estimates of how common shootings like the one at Newtown are. Using records obtained from journal articles, government and advocacy organization reports, and news stories, the Congressional Research Service reports that seventy-eight mass shootings occurred between 1983 and 2012. These shootings resulted in 547 deaths and 476 injuries. For the purposes of its report, the Congressional Research Service defined a mass shooting as a crime that occurs in a relatively public place and results in at least four deaths. However, some other estimates of mass shootings are far higher. For example, Everytown for Gun Safety, an organization working to end gun violence, analyzed shootings that resulted in at least four deaths per incident between January 2009 and July 2014. Included in the group's analysis are shootings that occurred in connection with domestic or family violence. It finds that in this five-and-a-half-year period, there were 110 shootings, which is almost 2 per month. In comparison, according to the most recent statistics from the Centers for Disease Control and Prevention (CDC), in the United States in 2011 alone, more than 10,000 gun-related homicides occurred—and none of these were classified as mass shootings.

In 2014 the FBI released a report on a more broadly defined category known as "active shooting incidents." In this report, an active shooting is defined as a situation in which an individual or individuals are "actively engaged in killing or attempting to kill people in a confined and populated area,"[4] regardless of the number of deaths that result. The FBI reports that between 2000 and 2013, there were 160 such incidents.

A Continuing Cycle

One thing common to most mass shootings that occur in the United States is the response that they provoke. Every time a shooting occurs, citizens are shocked and outraged. There are widespread demands that the government take action to ensure that such a tragedy does not occur again. Blame for shootings and calls for reform are usually centered on the same topics: the efficacy of gun laws, whether violent video games inspire shootings, whether the United States encourages a culture of violence that makes shootings more likely, and the risk of the mentally ill becoming shooters. These issues are all extremely controversial and have fervent supporters on all sides.

However, although calls for reform sometimes do lead to law changes such as stricter gun regulations in some states, the biggest impact of US mass shootings is simply to provoke more public debate. In 2013, following the Washington Navy Yard shooting in which thirteen people were killed, President Barack Obama worried that despite their outrage, Americans are not doing anything significant to stop mass shootings from occurring. He says, "It ought to be a shock to us all as a nation and as a people. It ought to obsess us. It ought to lead to some sort of transformation." However, he says that the reality is that very little changes:

> "Sometimes I fear there's a creeping resignation that these tragedies are just somehow the way it is, that this is somehow the new normal."[5]
>
> —Barack Obama is the forty-fourth president of the United States.

After the round-of-clock coverage on cable news, after the heartbreaking interviews with families, after all the speeches and all the punditry and all the commentary, nothing happens. Alongside the anguish of these American families, alongside the accumulated outrage so many of us feel, sometimes I fear there's a creeping resignation that these tragedies are just somehow the way it is, that this is somehow the new normal.[5]

No matter how one views the response to such shootings, most people agree that each and every one of these incidents represents a disturbing picture of modern life. And perhaps even more distressing is the thought that more such incidents are likely to occur.

Chapter One

Are Mass Shootings a Serious Problem?

Mass Shootings Are a Serious Problem

- Mass shootings are becoming more common.
- The threat of shootings is actually underestimated because many incidents are not covered in the media.
- Domestic violence–related mass shootings are a serious threat.
- School shootings are a serious problem.

The Debate at a Glance

Mass Shootings Are Not a Serious Problem

- Compared to other types of homicide, the occurrence of mass shootings is very small.
- There is no evidence that mass shootings are becoming more common.
- The public has overestimated the threat of mass shootings.
- The threat of school shootings has been exaggerated.

Mass Shootings Are a Serious Problem

"Mass shootings are all too common. And they have become increasingly deadly."

—Eric Holder is a former US attorney general.

Eric Holder, quoted in US Department of Justice, "Following Mass Shooting Incidents, Attorney General Holder Urges Congress to Approve $15 Million to Train Law Enforcement Officers for 'Active Shooting' Situations," press release, April 15, 2014. www.justice.gov.

Consider these questions as you read:

1. Do you agree that if mass shootings are becoming more frequent in the United States, then they are a serious problem? Why or why not?
2. How persuasive is the argument that mass shootings are a serious threat to Americans? Which arguments provide the strongest support for this perspective, and why?
3. How strong is the argument that school shootings are a serious problem in the United States? Explain your answer.

Editor's note: The discussion that follows presents common arguments made in support of this perspective, reinforced by facts, quotes, and examples taken from various sources.

On January 8, 2011, Mavanell and Dorwin Stoddard drove to a Tucson grocery store for a meet-and-greet event with Arizona representative Gabrielle Giffords. As the Stoddards stood outside the store, Jared Loughner suddenly walked up to the group and shot Giffords in the head. He then opened fire on the crowd, killing six people—including Dorwin—and wounding twelve others. At Loughner's sentencing hearing, Mavanell spoke about how Loughner's actions changed her life forever. She says that her husband was fatally shot as he fell on top of her to protect her and that he died in her arms. "You took away my life, my love, my reason for living," she said to Loughner, "I hate living without him. No one to hold me, no one to love me, no one to talk to, no one to care."[6] At the hearing, other victims testified about how their lives had also been irreversibly altered by Loughner's actions. Ron Barber, who was shot in the leg, said, "The physical and mental wounds will be with us forever."[7] Shootings such as this happen all too often in the United States, irrevocably changing and destroying lives. Clearly, mass shootings are a serious problem.

Becoming More Common

Analyses of shootings in the United States show that these events are becoming more common. In 2014 the FBI released a report on active shooting incidents. These are defined as situations in which an individual or individuals are actively engaged in killing or attempting to kill people in a confined and populated area. Not all the events studied by the FBI qualify as mass shootings because in some cases the number of fatalities was less than three; however, they all involved a shooter opening fire on a group of people. The FBI analyzed shootings over a fourteen-year period and found that the frequency of these events is increasing. According to the report, an average of 6.4 such incidents occurred annually between 2000 and 2006. That number increased to an average of 16.4 incidents annually between 2007 and 2013. As these statistics show, incidents of shooters firing at groups of people have more than doubled in the space of only fourteen years. The report illustrates a new reality—one that Americans need to prepare for. The report's authors say as much when they conclude: "Recognizing the increased active shooter threat and the swiftness with which active shooter incidents unfold, these study results support the importance of training and exercises—not only for law enforcement but also for citizens."[8]

"Over the last four years, America has witnessed an increase of nearly 150 percent in the number of people shot and killed in connection with active shooter incidents."[9]

—Eric Holder is a former US attorney general.

Not only are shooting incidents becoming more common, but more people are dying as a result of shootings. According to a 2012 report in *Mother Jones*, a news publication that has conducted extensive research into mass shootings, 2012 was the worst year for mass shootings in modern US history. A total of 151 people were injured and killed as a result of mass shootings that year. Former US attorney general Eric Holder also reports that shooting deaths have increased. He says, "Over the last four years, America has witnessed an increase of nearly 150 percent in the number of people shot and killed in connection with active shooter incidents."[9] Like the FBI, he recognizes that these events are a serious threat to Americans and advocates an increased focus on preventing them and responding effectively when they do occur.

Underreporting Shootings

If anything, mass shootings are more of a problem than people even realize. Some shootings get national media attention; for example, shootings in which a large number of people die or in which the deaths are particularly surprising or upsetting to the public. For instance, in the 2012 Sandy Hook Elementary School shooting, most of the victims were six- and seven-year-olds, and media coverage was extensive. However, there are many shootings that get much less notice, except maybe locally—such as ones that involve an estranged ex-spouse or other family member. J. Pete Blair, a Texas State University criminal justice professor, is coauthor of the 2014 FBI report about shootings. He says he was surprised at how many shooting incidents the researchers actually found. The number was higher than media coverage led him to believe. He says, "I think it speaks to the fact that while there is interest in the media, many incidents don't get covered, especially if they result in few injuries or don't draw the body count of others."[10]

> "While there is interest in the media, many incidents don't get covered, especially if they result in few injuries or don't draw the body count of others."[10]
>
> —J. Pete Blair is a Texas State University criminal justice professor and coauthor of a 2014 FBI report about shootings.

Mass Shootings Are a Serious Problem in the United States

These graphs show data from a Federal Bureau of Investigation study of active shooting incidents in the United States. An active shooting is defined as a situation where an individual or individuals are actively engaged in killing or attempting to kill people in a confined and populated area. The graphs show that the number of incidents and casualties (both deaths and injuries) has fluctuated between 2000 and 2013. However, the general trend is that active shooting incidents and casualties are both becoming more common.

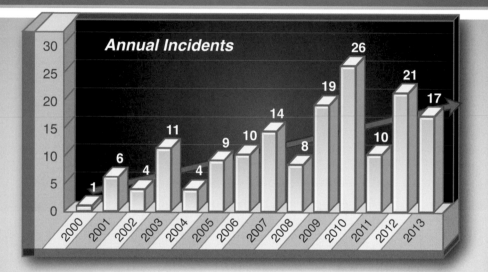

Annual Incidents

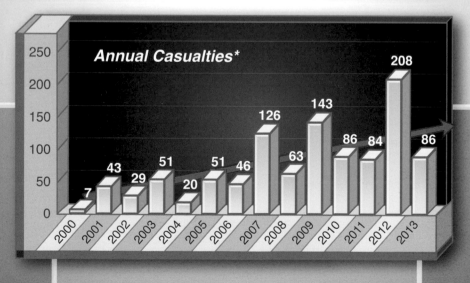

Annual Casualties*

*Casualties includes the number of people killed and wounded.

Source: J. Pete Blair and Katherine W. Schweit, "A Study of Active Shooter Incidents, 2000–2013," Texas State University and Federal Bureau of Investigation, US Department of Justice, Washington, DC, 2014. www.fbi.gov.

In fact, mass shootings that are triggered by domestic or family problems are a serious threat to people in the United States. Research shows that they are the most common type of mass shooting. For example, Everytown for Gun Safety, an organization working to end gun violence, analyzed shootings between January 2009 and July 2014 and found that in at least 57 percent of the incidents, one of the shooter's victims was a current or former spouse or partner or another family member. In another analysis, *USA Today* catalogued mass killings between 2007 and 2013 and found that almost half involved a person killing his or her family members. (The majority of these killings were shootings, but some involved other weapons.) *USA Today* explains that some of the common triggers for this type of killing are breakups, job losses, holiday stress, or financial ruin. For example, it cites a 2008 mass shooting in California:

> Facing a divorce and having lost his job, Bruce Pardo, 45, paid a seamstress to make him an extra-large Santa Claus suit. . . . On Christmas Eve, clad in the Santa outfit and carrying four guns and a device to spray fuel, he went to his ex-wife's parents' home, where her extended family had gathered. He barged in on the festivities just before midnight and began shooting, killing his ex, her parents, three siblings and two sisters-in-law.[11]

School Shootings

Mass shootings that occur in schools are also a serious problem. According to the Mass Shootings in America project by Stanford University Libraries, about 40 percent of mass shootings since 1996 have happened in school-related facilities. The 2014 FBI report states that educational facilities are the second-most common type of mass shooting location. In addition, it says that school shootings account for some of the higher number of casualties for the incidents it studied. The FBI reports:

> The highest death tolls among the 160 incidents occurred at Virginia Polytechnic Institute and State University in Blacksburg, Virginia (32 killed, 17 wounded) and Sandy Hook Elementary

School in Newtown, Connecticut (26 killed, 2 wounded [1 additional death at a residence]). Other high casualty counts occurred during the shootings at Northern Illinois University in DeKalb, Illinois (5 killed, 16 wounded) and Santana High School in Santee, California (2 killed, 13 wounded).[12]

Following the 2012 Sandy Hook Elementary School shooting, the White House issued a report about gun violence. The report maintains that the threat of mass shootings in schools is so serious that the United States needs to take action to make schools safer. The authors of the report stress that not only are too many lives lost in mass shootings in schools, but exposure to violence such as this can have a significant negative impact on survivors for the rest of their lives. These negative effects include harm to mental health and development and a substantially increased risk that students will later engage in violent acts themselves. The authors insist, "If even one child's life can be saved, then we need to act."[13]

An Increasingly Deadly Threat

Like the 2014 FBI report, the White House report stresses the importance of additional training for law enforcement, first responders, and others most likely to approach mass shooting situations. Unfortunately, mass shootings are a regular and increasingly common occurrence in the United States that necessitate greater awareness and preparedness like this. They alter the lives of a significant number of people every year, and they are a serious problem.

Mass Shootings Are Not a Serious Problem

"While tragic and shocking, public mass shootings account for few of the murders related to firearms that occur annually in the United States."

—Jerome P. Bjelopera is a specialist in organized crime and terrorism for the Congressional Research Service.

Jerome P. Bjelopera et al. "Public Mass Shootings in the United States: Selected Implications for Federal Public Health and Safety Policy," Congressional Research Service, March 18, 2013. http://fas.org.

Consider these questions as you read:

1. Do you agree with the argument that most people will never become the victims of a mass shooting? Why or why not?
2. How strong is the argument that people tend to have an exaggerated perception of the risk of mass shootings? Explain.
3. In addition to making people believe that shootings are more likely than they really are, can you think of any ways that excessive media coverage of mass shootings might be harmful?

Editor's note: The discussion that follows presents common arguments made in support of this perspective, reinforced by facts, quotes, and examples taken from various sources.

Gun-related violence and death are extremely common in the United States. In fact, researchers estimate that the nation has one of the highest rates of gun-related deaths of all developed countries. However, whereas people being killed by firearms is a frequent problem, mass shootings are not. Research shows that mass shootings actually account for less than 1 percent of all gun-related deaths in the United States. The real problem is not this miniscule percentage, but the factors that cause the other 99 percent of America's gun deaths. Suicide accounts for a large percentage of these deaths. In 2010 the CDC reports that there were about 31,000 gun deaths in the United States; more than half, or about 19,000 of them, were suicides. In comparison, according to an analysis by the publication *Mother Jones*, in 2010 the total number of people injured and killed in mass shootings was less than twenty. Mass shootings are often far more shocking to the public than suicides, and they often receive national attention. However, as these numbers show, although any shooting death is a tragic occurrence, the reality is that mass shootings are not a serious problem for most Americans.

Not a Real Threat for Most People

Another way to put the threat of mass shootings in perspective is to compare the number of mass shootings to the total number of homicides that occur each year. Josh Blackman is an assistant professor at the South Texas College of Law. He uses homicide statistics to do this, showing just how small the number of mass shooting deaths really is compared to all homicides that happen every year in the United States. Blackman says, "The Bureau of Justice Statistics reported that from 2002–2011, 95 percent of total homicide incidents involved a single fatality, 4 percent involved two victims, 0.6 percent involved 3 victims, and *only .02 percent* involved four or more victims. . . . In other words, the bottom line is that out of every 10,000 incidents of homicide, roughly two are mass killings."[14]

> "While every senseless massacre leaves a community in shock and tragically cuts short too many lives, the vast majority of Americans will remain untouched."[15]
>
> —Laura Smith-Spark is a journalist.

As terrible as mass shootings are, they are a rare occurrence. They simply do not represent a serious threat to most people. As CNN journalist Laura Smith-Spark says, "While every senseless massacre leaves a community in shock and tragically cuts short too many lives, the vast majority of Americans will remain untouched apart from the screaming headlines."[15]

No Evidence of an Increasing Trend

Not only are mass shootings a relatively minor problem compared to other types of gun violence, but there is no evidence that they are becoming more common. Journalist Jesse Walker has analyzed various mass shooting estimates in order to understand the overall trend, and he reports, "Over the decades the number of these murders has zig-zagged up and down without a discernable pattern."[16] For example, 2012 was a year with a large number of mass shootings; however, this does not mean they are becoming more frequent. It just means that 2012 was a bad year amid other, much less violent years.

In fact, researchers may be overestimating the number of mass shootings that have occurred in recent years. This is because news reports are now more easily available than in the past. Digital sources make it easy for researchers to find shooting reports. In comparison, information about older shootings might not be so easily accessible. Criminologist James Alan Fox argues, "If you go back to those earlier years, I don't think they've gotten them all."[17]

An Exaggerated Perception of Risk

The overall perception that mass shootings are increasing and that Americans are at grave risk of becoming victims of such shootings is erroneous but common. Most people have an exaggerated perception of the risk of mass shootings. They incorrectly perceive them to be a far greater threat than they really are. There are a number of psychological explanations for this. One is that because a mass shooting is both unfamiliar and horrifying, people tend to perceive it as more dangerous. More familiar threats—for instance, the threat of being in a car accident—are incorrectly perceived as less of a danger than a shooting. Forensic psychiatrist Park Dietz conducted a study of New York subway riders that illustrates this phenomenon. His interviews with riders revealed that many were afraid of being pushed off the subway platform in front of a train, even though this type of crime is extremely rare. In the same way, many people worry about mass shootings, even though they are unlikely ever to become a victim of

Mass Shootings Comprise a Fraction of US Gun Violence

Although mass shootings attract a lot of media and public attention, they represent less than 1 percent of homicides involving three or more victims. This graph shows the number of multiple-victim homicides (most involving guns) that have occurred each year in the United States between 1980 and 2008. As frightening as mass shootings are, these statistics illustrate that few people will ever die in a mass shooting.

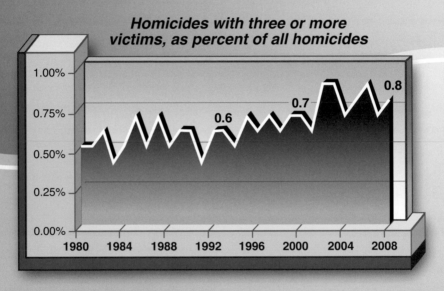

Homicides with three or more victims, as percent of all homicides

Source: Pew Research Center, "Mass Shootings Rivet National Attention, but Are a Small Share of Gun Violence," September 17, 2013. www.pewresearch.org.

one. "This is statistically rare and should not be in the forefront of everyone's mind as they go about their day," Dietz says. "But it's unavoidable."[18]

Another reason is that people often focus their attention on the similarities they have with shooting victims, and that makes the possibility of a shooting seem more likely. Many shootings happen in locations that the majority of people frequent, like schools or businesses. The result is that because these locations, and the people in them, are all very familiar to most people, it is easy to imagine being in that same situation. As criminologist Grant Duwe says, "There is this feeling that could have been me. It makes it so much more frightening."[19]

Another reason for the exaggerated perception of risk is the extensive media coverage that often follows a mass shooting. Some shootings dominate the news for days, with investigations into the possible motives of the shooters, reports about the victims and their families, and extensive debate about how to prevent another shooting from happening. In addition, there are often references to prior shootings. Film critic Roger Ebert commented on this in relation to the 1999 Columbine shooting, where two teenagers killed thirteen people. He says, "When an unbalanced kid walks into a school and starts shooting, it becomes a major media event. Cable news drops ordinary programming and goes around the clock with it. The story is assigned a logo and a theme song."[20] The popularity of social media amplifies this effect. The result of all this attention is that the public becomes so focused on mass shootings that it tends to perceive them as far more common and threatening than they really are.

The Threat of School Shootings Is Exaggerated

School shootings are an especially emotional topic—and understandably so. But the reality is that the threat of school shootings has been greatly exaggerated. Dewey Cornell is a clinical psychologist and a professor at the University of Virginia. He says, "I know on the heels of any school shooting, there's the perception that violence is on the rise. It's not. In fact, there's been a very steady downward trend for the past 15 years."[21]

Stephen Brock, an expert on school violence, agrees that the chance of a student being harmed in a shooting or any other type of crime at school is small. In fact, he says, "It's clear that schools are the safest place for a student to be."[22] Statistics back this up. A 2013 report by the National Center for Education Statistics shows that less than 2 percent of youth homicides occur at school. Everytown

> "I know on the heels of any school shooting, there's the perception that violence is on the rise. It's not. In fact, there's been a very steady downward trend for the past 15 years."[21]
>
> —Dewey Cornell is a clinical psychologist and a professor at the University of Virginia.

for Gun Safety analyzed mass shootings between January 2009 and July 2014 and found that only 4 out of 110 mass shootings occurred in schools during those years.

Statistically Rare

Although many people worry about the threat of mass shootings, the evidence shows that much of this worry is unfounded. Sociology professor Glenn Muschert observes, "These events occupy a bigger portion of our perception of risk than they probably should."[23] Americans should be aware that shootings are actually rare compared to the various other risks they face. For example, a person is much more likely to be injured or killed in a car accident than in a mass shooting. Overall, the evidence shows that mass shootings are not a serious problem in the United States.

Chapter Two

Will Stricter Gun Control Reduce Mass Shootings?

Stricter Gun Control Will Reduce Mass Shootings

- Some shootings can be prevented by reducing the number of guns in the United States.
- Closing background check loopholes would make it harder for dangerous people to obtain guns.
- Mass shooting casualties will be reduced by banning certain types of guns and ammunition.
- Research shows that tighter restrictions reduce shooting deaths.

The Debate at a Glance

Stricter Gun Control Will Not Reduce Mass Shootings

- Stricter laws will make it more difficult for citizens to protect themselves from shooters.
- Mass shooters will obtain guns no matter what regulations are in place.
- Stricter gun control would violate the Second Amendment.
- Research shows that there is no correlation between gun ownership rates and violent crime like shootings.

Stricter Gun Control Will Reduce Mass Shootings

"Americans overwhelmingly support background checks and reasonable restrictions on gun ownership. Failing to take action will inevitably lead to other senseless—and preventable—tragedies."

—Colin Goddard is a survivor of the 2007 mass shooting at Virginia Tech.

Colin Goddard, comment on *New York Times Upfront*, "Is It Too Easy to Get a Gun?," November 19, 2012. http://upfront.scholastic.com.

Consider these questions as you read:

1. Do you think it would be possible to enforce background checks for all gun sales in the United States? Why or why not?
2. Do you agree with the argument that banning certain types of guns and ammunition is an effective way to address mass shootings? Explain your answer.
3. How strong is the argument that stricter gun control laws will reduce mass shootings? Which argument do you think is the most persuasive? Why?

Editor's note: The discussion that follows presents common arguments made in support of this perspective, reinforced by facts, quotes, and examples taken from various sources.

On September 14, 2013, former US Navy sailor Aaron Alexis walked into a Virginia gun store and, after passing a background check, purchased a 12-gauge shotgun and two boxes of shells. Two days later he entered a bathroom in the Washington, DC, Navy Yard and assembled the gun. He then came out and opened fire, killing twelve people before he was killed by police. After the shooting, investigations into Alexis's past revealed that he had a history of violent behavior and negligent behavior with guns.

26

For example, in 2004 he was questioned by police for allegedly shooting out the tires of another person's vehicle, and in 2010 he was questioned for firing a gun into a neighboring apartment after a dispute over noise.

Nevertheless, Alexis had no trouble buying a gun. This is a problem. Buying a gun in America is too easy. People such as Alexis who have demonstrated that they are not fit to own a gun should not be able to buy one. "There is no other civilized society that would allow him to legally own a gun and carry it in public," says Ladd Everitt, communications director for the Coalition to Stop Gun Violence. Current gun laws are simply not adequate. "We have a regulatory system in this country that is riddled with loopholes and a joke,"[24] Everitt adds. To prevent future mass shootings like that which occurred at the navy yard, gun control laws must be tightened.

> "We have a regulatory system in this country that is riddled with loopholes and a joke."[24]
>
> —Ladd Everitt is communications director for the Coalition to Stop Gun Violence.

Too Many Guns

America simply has too many guns in private hands, and there are too few obstacles to mentally unstable people obtaining guns. By most estimates, the United States has the highest rate of gun ownership per capita in the world. Overall, approximately 300 million guns are privately owned, almost one for every person in the country. According to the Small Arms Survey, an internationally recognized source of information about firearms, the United States has less than 5 percent of the world's population but 35 to 50 percent of its guns. People with criminal records or mental health issues have no business buying guns. Laws intended to prevent such purchases simply have too many loopholes. Federal law currently requires background checks of potential gun buyers, except in the case of sales between private individuals. The problem here is that almost 40 percent of gun sales occur through private sellers, says a 2013 White House report. This means that close to half of gun purchasers are not screened for a criminal record or any other indication that they should not be allowed to purchase a gun. Many of these private sales occur at gun shows, where vendors often sell a gun to anyone who wants it.

Colin Goddard is a survivor of the 2007 mass shooting at Virginia Tech in Blacksburg, Virginia, and he works for the Brady Center to Prevent Gun Violence. He says, "I've gone to gun shows in Virginia, Minnesota, Ohio, and Texas and bought handguns, Tec-9's, Mac-11's, shotguns, rifles, even an AK-47—all without undergoing a background check to determine whether I should be allowed to buy a firearm."[25] New York City has conducted undercover investigations at gun shows in Arizona, Nevada, Tennessee, and Ohio and found that more than half of sellers would even sell to people who actually told them they probably couldn't pass a background check. This is a clear example of why background checks should be required for all guns sales, regardless of whether they are public or private.

Ban Certain Types of Firearms

A ban on certain types of firearms and ammunition would also go a long way toward reducing casualties in a mass shooting. In many such shootings, deaths and injuries are high specifically because the shooter used semiautomatic weapons and/or high-capacity ammunition. Certain types of semiautomatic firearms—also known as assault weapons—allow the shooter to quickly and easily fire many bullets. High-capacity ammunition clips allow them to fire more shots before they have to stop and reload. Banning these types of guns and ammunition would help save lives. In an analysis of the weapons used in mass shootings between 1982 and 2012, news publication *Mother Jones* finds that more than half of the shooters had assault weapons, high-capacity magazines, or both. David Chipman, a former special agent in the Bureau of Alcohol, Tobacco, Firearms and Explosives, discusses the high-capacity magazine in particular and argues that it increases the damage a shooter can inflict. He says, "It turns a killer into a killing machine."[26]

> "[A high-capacity magazine] turns a killer into a killing machine."[26]
>
> —David Chipman is a former special agent in the Bureau of Alcohol, Tobacco, Firearms and Explosives.

Banning Assault Weapons and High-Capacity Magazines Would Reduce Shooting Casualties

Semiautomatic weapons (often referred to as assault weapons) and high-capacity magazines allow rapid firing and many shots—features that heighten the likelihood of many victims. A ban on these types of weapons would go a long way toward reducing casualties in mass shootings. This can be seen in statistics compiled by Everytown for Gun Safety, an organization that is working to end gun violence in the United States. According to the group's 2014 report, assault weapons or high-capacity magazines were used in about 13 percent of mass shootings between January 2009 and July 2014. In the cases that involved these weapons, 156 percent more people were shot, and 63 percent more died, than in other mass shootings.

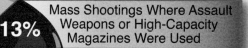

13% Mass Shootings Where Assault Weapons or High-Capacity Magazines Were Used

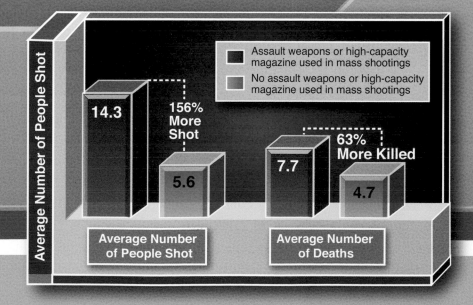

Average Number of People Shot

- Assault weapons or high-capacity magazine used in mass shootings
- No assault weapons or high-capacity magazine used in mass shootings

14.3 — 156% More Shot — 5.6

Average Number of People Shot

7.7 — 63% More Killed — 4.7

Average Number of Deaths

Source: Everytown for Gun Safety, "Analysis of Recent Mass Shootings," July 2014. https://s3.amazonaws.com.

In the 2012 Sandy Hook Elementary School shooting, Adam Lanza used a semiautomatic Bushmaster rifle with devastating effects. It allowed him to kill twenty-six people in about ten minutes. H. Wayne Carver II, chief medical examiner for the state of Connecticut, explains that Lanza was able to shoot most of the victims more than once, and he inflicted an extreme amount of damage in this short amount of time. Carver says, "I've been at this for a third of a century. My sensibilities may not be the average man, but this probably is the worst I have seen or the worst that I know of any of my colleagues having seen."[27] On the same day that Lanza went on his shooting spree, thirty-six-year-old Min Yongjun attacked students in a Chinese school. However, whereas Lanza killed twenty-six people, none died in the attack in China. The *Economist* points out that the weapon used was an important difference. It says, "The American was armed with a semi-automatic rifle with an extended magazine and two semi-automatic handguns. Every country has its madmen, but Min was armed only with a knife, so none of his victims died."[28]

More Restrictions Will Help Reduce Casualties

Most people concede that tighter gun laws will not stop every individual intent on harming others. However, it is possible to reduce casualties when shootings like these occur. Filmmaker James Stern directed *All the Rage*, a movie about US gun violence. He argues that more restrictive laws can make a significant difference in situations where angry or disturbed individuals try to harm others. He illustrates his argument with a personal experience: "When I was a kid in sixth grade, there was a kid who was bullied. He was overweight. He came to school to seek vengeance (and brought a butcher knife. He chased the kids around and couldn't catch them)." Stern points out that if the youth had been armed with a gun instead of a knife, the result might have been quite different. "If he came to school with an assault weapon, those kids would have been dead."[29]

Australia's experience with gun laws lends support to this theory. In 1996 a gunman there killed thirty-five people and wounded eighteen others. Following this shooting, Australia significantly tightened its gun laws, and the result has been a reduction in shooting deaths there. Law changes included banning certain guns and making it much more difficult to purchase a gun. In addition, the government purchased hundreds of thousands of guns from civilian owners and received thousands more in voluntary surrender, significantly reducing the number of privately owned guns. Ten years after these changes, researchers investigated the effect. Their study, published in the journal *Injury Prevention*, reveals that in the eighteen years before the reforms, thirteen mass shootings took place in Australia, whereas in the ten and a half years after the reforms were enacted, no mass shootings occurred.

More Guns Is Not the Solution

Some gun control critics insist that stricter laws are a mistake because they make it more difficult for law-abiding citizens to purchase and use guns in order to defend themselves from shooters. However, in reality there is no evidence that arming citizens is an effective way to stop shootings. News publication *Mother Jones* has conducted extensive research into mass shootings, and *Mother Jones* journalist Mark Follman reports that in the sixty-two mass shootings that have occurred in the past thirty years, not a single shooting has been stopped by an armed civilian. In fact, rather than stopping shooters, armed civilians are more likely to harm themselves or innocent bystanders. Follman explains, "For their part, law enforcement officials overwhelmingly hate the idea of armed civilians getting involved. As a senior FBI agent told me, it would make their jobs more difficult if they had to figure out which of the shooters at an active crime scene was the bad guy. And . . . the danger to innocent bystanders from ordinary civilians whipping out firearms is obvious."[30]

Overall, the evidence shows that easy access to guns is placing people at an increased risk for mass shootings. The United States could reduce this threat by significantly tightening its gun control laws.

Stricter Gun Control Will Not Reduce Mass Shootings

"[New] laws won't stop these attacks from occurring."

—John Lott is a gun policy researcher.

John Lott, "New Gun Laws Will Do Nothing to Stop Mass Shooting Attacks," *Fox News*, July 30, 2012. www.foxnews.com.

Consider these questions as you read:

1. Do you agree with the argument that guns can protect Americans from mass shooters? Why or why not?
2. Do you agree with gun control critics who argue that laws are irrelevant to mass shooters? Why or why not?
3. Taking into account the facts and ideas presented in this discussion, how persuasive is the argument that stricter gun control will not reduce mass shootings? Which facts and ideas are strongest, and why?

Editor's note: The discussion that follows presents common arguments made in support of this perspective, reinforced by facts, quotes, and examples taken from various sources.

Every year Gallup conducts polls regarding Americans' attitudes towards gun policies. Although gun control advocates are extremely vocal about tightening regulations, these Gallup polls show that people are actually divided about gun control. In general, there is not a clear majority in favor of stricter regulations. In fact, significant percentages are satisfied with current laws and do not believe changes are needed. For example, in a 2014 poll, Gallup found that 40 percent of respondents are totally satisfied with the nation's laws and policies on guns. Only 31 percent said they believe laws should be stricter. In previous years the percentage of those satisfied with the laws was even higher: 43 percent in 2013 and 50 percent in 2012. As these percentages show, a large number of Americans do not believe stricter gun control is necessary. While critics argue that it is the best way to reduce mass shootings, the evidence actually shows that tightening gun laws would be both ineffective and dangerous.

Guns Needed for Deterrence and Protection

The threat of mass shooters will always exist. This is sad fact of modern society. As National Rifle Association vice president Wayne LaPierre noted in a press conference after the 2012 Sandy Hook Elementary School shooting, "Our society is populated by an unknown number of genuine monsters—people so deranged, so evil, so possessed by voices and driven by demons that no sane person can possibly *ever* comprehend them. They walk among us every day."[31]

Because it is impossible to identify these dangerous individuals before they commit violence, it is essential to always be prepared to protect oneself and others. The best way to reduce mass shootings is not to restrict guns, but to increase the ability of the general population to acquire and carry them. As LaPierre states, "The *only* thing that stops a *bad* guy with a gun is a *good* guy with a gun. Would you rather have your 911 call bring a good guy with a gun from *a mile* away . . . or *a minute* away?"[32]

A 1997 shooting illustrates this point. In that situation seventeen-year-old Luke Woodham stabbed his mother to death with a butcher knife, then drove to his Mississippi high school and opened fire on students and teachers. When he heard gunfire, assistant principal Joel Myrick hurried to his truck in the school parking lot and took out the pistol he kept there. He ran after Woodham and used the pistol to hold him at bay. Two students were killed, and seven more wounded by Woodham's rampage; however, those numbers would likely have been higher if Myrick had not been armed and able to stop him.

> "The *only* thing that stops a *bad* guy with a gun is a *good* guy with a gun."[32]
>
> —Wayne LaPierre is vice president of the National Rifle Association.

Protection is not the only reason to avoid harsher gun laws. Deterrence is also an important factor. If potential shooters know that members of the public are armed and willing to shoot back, they would be far less likely to engage in such deviant behavior. Gun policy researcher John Lott explains, "You can deter criminality by making it riskier for people to commit crimes. And one way to make it riskier is to create the impression among the criminal population that the law-abiding citizen they want to target may have a gun."[33] Gun-free areas such as schools simply increase the chance of a mass shooting because a would-be shooter knows there will be nobody to stop them. Mike Hammond, legislative counsel for the Gun Owners of America, argues that this is what happened in the 2012 Sandy Hook shooting. He says, "When federal law advertised the fact that [Adam] Lanza could walk into school, shoot up a kindergarten, get his name on the evening news and not risk the possibility that anyone was going to fire back, that pretty much guaranteed the result."[34]

Obtaining Guns Despite the Laws

Like it or not, gun laws in the United States clearly have not achieved their goal, which is to prevent dangerous people from obtaining guns. More laws or harsher laws are simply not going to improve this outcome. People intent on committing crimes or hurting others will always find a way to get guns. James Alan Fox is the Lipman Family Professor of Criminology, Law, and Public Policy at Northeastern University in Boston. He explains that most mass shooters are strongly driven to kill and thus very resourceful at finding the weapons they need. He says, "Mass killers are determined, deliberate and dead-set on murder. They plan methodically to execute their victims, finding the means no matter what laws or other impediments the state attempts to place in their way. To them, the will to kill cannot be denied."[35]

A 2012 shooting, in which a Wisconsin man shot and killed his estranged wife and two other people at a salon and spa where she worked, is a

> "Mass killers are determined, deliberate and dead-set on murder. . . . To them, the will to kill cannot be denied."[35]
>
> —James Alan Fox is the Lipman Family Professor of Criminology, Law, and Public Policy at Northeastern University in Boston.

case in point. Radcliffe Haughton had reportedly threatened and terrorized his wife numerous times before the shooting, and as a result she had taken out a restraining order against him. The court order meant that he could not come near her, and a restraining order also prohibited him from buying a gun. However, according to news reports, he did so with relative ease through the website ArmsList.com, then used that gun in the shooting.

The Second Amendment

Not only would stricter laws not reduce mass shootings, but they would violate constitutional freedom. The Second Amendment to the US Constitution guarantees the right of US citizens to own and carry guns without interference from the government. The amendment reads, "A well regulated Militia, being necessary to the security of a free State, the right of the people to keep and bear Arms, shall not be infringed." When this was written, Americans strongly believed that citizens should be guaranteed certain basic rights, and that one of those rights is the ability to own a gun for self-defense and for protection in the case of government oppression. The Second Amendment was made part of the Constitution to ensure that this right was never taken away.

Various groups have tried repeatedly to whittle away this right. Supreme Court rulings in 2008 and 2010 affirmed it, however. In the 2010 decision, the court ruled that a law prohibiting Chicago residents from purchasing a handgun for personal home defense was unconstitutional. The decision states, "It is clear that the Framers [of the Constitution] . . . counted the right to keep and bear arms among those fundamental rights necessary to our system of ordered liberty."[36] Laws that make it harder for law-abiding citizens to own and carry guns clearly violate this important constitutional right.

No Relationship Between Gun Ownership and Violent Crime

Those who argue that mass shootings are common in the United States because of the number of guns in circulation need to examine the facts.

Most People Do Not Favor Stricter Gun Control

No responsible person wants to see another mass shooting. But passing more stringent gun laws is not the way to reduce such shootings. This is borne out in a series of polls done by the Gallup organization. Those polls, conducted between 2001 and 2014, reveal that, on average, about 5 percent of respondents are satisfied with US gun laws and policies. Among those dissatisfied, only about one-third support stronger gun laws.

Survey participants were asked if they were satisfied or dissatisfied with the nation's gun laws or policies. Those who said they were dissatisfied were then asked whether they would like to see US gun laws made more strict, less strict, or remain as they are.

	Total satisfied %	Dissatisfied, more strict %	Dissatisfied, less strict %	Dissatisfied, remain same %	No opinion %
Jan 2014	40	31	16	8	5
Jan 2013	43	38	5	8	5
Jan 2012	50	25	8	9	8
Jan 2008	49	30	8	6	7
Jan 2007	50	30	6	7	7
Jan 2006	47	32	7	4	9
Jan 2005	51	32	6	5	6
Jan 2004	51	33	6	6	4
Jan 2003	47	32	9	6	6
Jan 2002	48	33	8	6	5
Jan 2001	38	39	9	9	6

Source: Gallup, "Guns," October 7, 2014. www.gallup.com.

Gun violence in general, and mass shootings in particular, have many causes—and gun ownership is not one of them. This can be seen by looking at other countries. Journalist Kevin D. Williamson explains:

> If you take the 20 countries with the highest rates of private gun ownership, you'll see some very dangerous and high-crime places (Yemen and Iraq), some places with relatively high crime (the United States), and a lot of low-crime countries (Switzerland, Sweden, Norway, Canada). If you take the countries with the fewest guns per capita, you'll see some very safe, low-crime places (Singapore, Japan) and some truly outstanding places to get murdered (Haiti, Rwanda, Sierra Leone).[37]

Thomas Sowell, a senior fellow at the Hoover Institution, uses examples from within the United States to show additional evidence that more guns do not necessarily mean more crime. He reports that communities and populations with the most guns frequently have lower murder rates than other areas. For example, he says, "The rate of gun ownership is higher in rural areas, but the murder rate is higher in urban areas. The rate of gun ownership is higher among whites than among blacks, but the murder rate is higher among blacks."[38] From these facts, one can clearly see that culture, not the availability of guns, is the strongest factor influencing the occurrence of mass shootings.

Stricter gun control is not the solution to the problem of mass shootings in the United States. The fact is that mass shooters are unlikely to be stopped by law changes because they act in complete disregard for the law. Politician Mitt Romney made this point while commenting on the 2012 shooting in Aurora, Colorado, where James Holmes killed twelve people and wounded fifty-eight. He points out, "A lot of what this young man did was clearly against the law. But the fact that it was against the law did not prevent it from happening."[39] There is widespread evidence that stricter laws will simply be ignored by shooters and will actually make the problem worse by preventing citizens from defending themselves.

Chapter Three

Do Violent Video Games Cause Mass Shootings?

Violent Video Games Cause Mass Shootings

- Numerous studies show that violent games cause aggression and violence.
- Games teach violence through repetition and rewards.
- Violent games falsely teach that violent behavior has no harmful consequences.
- There is evidence that some shooters are imitating video games.

The Debate at a Glance

Violent Video Games Do Not Cause Mass Shootings

- There is no evidence that violent video games cause violent behavior.
- Thousands of people around the world play games and never become mass shooters.
- Violent game play is often an expression of personal problems, not a cause of them.
- Violent games help prevent violence by letting players harmlessly release their frustrations.

Violent Video Games Cause Mass Shootings

"Clearly, not all violent gamers become mass killers. But these days, almost all nonterrorist mass shooters are violent gamers. The link is undeniable."

—Paul Sperry is a journalist.

Paul Sperry, "Restrict 'Columbine Simulators' and Violent Video Games Before Guns," *Investors.com*, December 19, 2012. http://news.investors.com.

Consider these questions as you read:

1. How persuasive is the argument that aggressive thoughts and actions can lead to violent behavior, including a mass shooting?
2. Do you agree with the argument that video games are an effective teaching tool for possible shooters? Why or why not?
3. Some people believe that video games teach players that shooting other people is harmless entertainment. Do you agree or disagree? Explain.

Editor's note: The discussion that follows presents common arguments made in support of this perspective, reinforced by facts, quotes, and examples taken from various sources.

In 2011 Norwegian Anders Behring Breivik shot and killed sixty-nine people—most of them teenagers—at a Norwegian Labour Party camp on Utøya Island. Witnesses later testified that Brevik was unemotional and methodical during the shooting. He ignored pleas for mercy and made sure those who tried to escape his attention by playing dead did not succeed. At his trial he testified about finding two girls hiding in a room. "One person put her head on the piano and I was sure she was pretend-ing. I saw another person pretending she was dead. And then I changed the magazine and shot both of them in the head."[40] At the trial he also revealed that he used the violent video game *Call of Duty* to train for the shooting. This game includes scenarios that involve shooting numerous people without emotion or mercy, just as Breivik did in real life. Closer investigation reveals that Breivik is not the only mass shooter to have been influenced by violent video games. There is evidence that violent video game play is a contributing factor in many mass shootings.

Evidence That Violent Games Cause Aggression and Violence

Researchers have studied gamers in the laboratory to find out how these games affect their thoughts and actions. The findings of these studies repeatedly show that violent video games cause real-world aggression and violent behavior. In 2010 well-known game researcher Craig A. Anderson and other experts conducted a major review of more than 130 existing studies. Their findings: a strong link exists between violent games and aggressive thinking and behavior. "The main findings can be succinctly summarized," they conclude. "Playing violent games causes an increase in the likelihood of physically aggressive behavior, aggressive affect, physiological arousal, and desensitization."[41] Their findings apply to both male and female gamers in the United States and other countries.

The results of a long-term study of video game effects among Singapore students also support this finding. Researchers studied 3,034 young people for three years. They found that youth who played violent games were more likely to have aggressive fantasies and attitudes and to engage in aggressive behavior such as hitting other people.

Teaching Violence

Violent games also teach players to see violence as a normal way to act and an effective way to solve problems. Young people do a lot of learning through observation. The Media Violence Commission explains that the human brain is wired to imitate what it sees. It says, "It is clear that people, and particularly young children, tend to mimic whatever they see others doing. We are fortunate to have this mimicry mechanism, as it promotes the rapid acquisition of all sorts of important skills."[42]

Violent Games Are Associated with Violent Behavior

Many people believe that violent video games cause violent behavior, including in some cases, mass shootings. They argue that youth in particular should be protected from this negative influence. This chart shows the results of a poll of 2,278 US adults concerning their beliefs about how violent video games affect youth. Most agree that there is a strong link between violent games and violent behavior. In addition, a significant percentage believes there should be government regulation of these games in order to protect youth from that negative influence.

"How much do you agree with the following statements?"

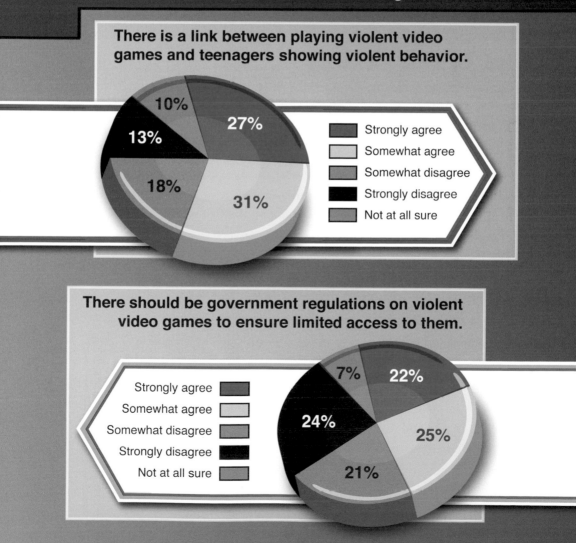

There is a link between playing violent video games and teenagers showing violent behavior.

- 10%
- 27%
- 13%
- 18%
- 31%

Legend:
- Strongly agree
- Somewhat agree
- Somewhat disagree
- Strongly disagree
- Not at all sure

There should be government regulations on violent video games to ensure limited access to them.

Legend:
- Strongly agree
- Somewhat agree
- Somewhat disagree
- Strongly disagree
- Not at all sure

- 7%
- 22%
- 24%
- 25%
- 21%

Source: Harris Interactive, "Majority of Americans See Connection Between Video Games and Violent Behavior in Teens," February 27, 2013. www.harrisinteractive.com.

However, in addition to positive behavior, people also mimic negative behaviors. In many violent games, players shoot and kill other people. Thus, they learn to see such behavior as normal and acceptable, and in some cases they will imitate that behavior in real life.

Overall, researchers have discovered that video games are excellent teachers. For this reason, games are often used in the classroom to teach skills such as math. However, just as math games are highly effective at teaching math, violent video games are highly effective at teaching violence. Players are frequently praised and rewarded for violence within such games. As researcher Brad Bushman explains, "You get points when you kill people. If you kill enough people, you get to advance to the next level of the game. You are also rewarded through things that you might hear. If you kill somebody, maybe you hear, 'Impressive, nice shot, you are tied for the lead.' And you hear these—praise, and we know that reinforcement increases the probability of behavior."[43] In addition, many people spend large amounts of time playing video games, and repetition further reinforces any learning that takes place.

> "[Some of my patients] think that what they see on TV with these video games, with the movies, is that you kill them and you get another life."[44]
>
> —Laura Davies is a child and adolescent psychiatrist in San Francisco.

A False Portrayal of Reality

The other lesson that frequent players learn is that violence, especially shooting and killing other people, is harmless entertainment. Killing is trivialized and even made to seem normal. This belies the seriousness of such acts in real life—and the dire consequences for both shooters and victims. Repeated play can also lead young people to develop a distorted view of reality and death. Laura Davies, a child and adolescent psychiatrist in San Francisco, says, "When I interview kids in my forensic practice, and they've killed somebody, they don't think the person is going to stay dead." Instead, she says, "They think that what they see on TV with these video games, with the movies, is that you kill them and you get another life."[44]

An Important Factor

Violent video games might not be the sole cause of real-world violence, but in many cases they are a serious contributing factor. That does not mean that every person who plays these games will go on a shooting rampage. Bushman says, "No doubt, most players don't become violent. That's because they come from good homes, aren't victims of bullying, don't have mental health issues, and don't have many of the other risk factors for violence." However, he argues that for people who are not so fortunate, violent games could be a serious risk factor. He says, "What about players who already are predisposed to violence? . . . They have a lot going against them, such as mental illness. Violent video games are just one more factor that may be pushing them toward violence."[45]

> "Violent video games are just one more factor that may be pushing . . . [some people] toward violence."[45]
>
> —Brad Bushman is a professor of communication and psychology at Ohio State University and has conducted numerous research studies on the effects of violent video games.

Peter Langman, a psychologist in Allentown, Pennsylvania, has studied mass shooters and agrees that although violent games are not a problem for the majority of people, for some disturbed individuals they are an inspiration. He says, "Those really vulnerable kids . . . are the ones who will take a movie or video game that 10 million other kids would watch and play and take as a guide for how to live their lives."[46]

Imitating Video Games

The theory that video games inspire some individuals to commit mass shootings is supported by the games themselves. In numerous such incidents, the shooters appeared to be imitating video games they played often. For example, in 1999 Colorado teenagers Dylan Klebold and Eric Harris went on a shooting rampage at Columbine High School, killing thirteen people and injuring more than twenty. Prior to the shooting, the two youths reportedly spent large amounts of time playing *Doom* and other violent video games, and many people believe that aspects of the shooting were modeled after the game. Following the shooting, investigators discovered a videotape that the youths had made in which they talk about what they planned to do. *Time* magazine reports on some of the links with gaming that are revealed in the video: "Eric Harris adjusts his video camera a few feet away, then settles into his chair with a bottle of Jack Daniels and a sawed-off shotgun in his lap. He calls it Arlene, after a favorite character in the gory *Doom* video games and books that he likes so much."[47] Later in the tape, Harris talks about their plans, and says, "It's going to be like [expletive] *Doom*."[48]

Every year, too many people die as a result of mass shootings, and society struggles to understand why these massacres happen and how to prevent them in the future. It is very difficult to predict or control most of the factors that seem to contribute to mass shootings, but violent games may be different. Bushman argues, "We have some control over violent video games. We can make it more difficult to get access to them. We can strengthen our laws against teens acquiring these games. Parents can keep the games out of their homes and help their children avoid them at friends' houses."[49] By recognizing that violent games are a cause of mass shootings, society can take preventative actions such as these to reduce the number of people who die in these tragedies every year.

Violent Video Games Do Not Cause Mass Shootings

"The reality is that there is no evidence linking violent games to mass shootings."

—Christopher J. Ferguson, well-known video games researcher.

Christopher J. Ferguson, "Video Games Didn't Cause Newtown Rampage," CNN, February 20, 2013. www.cnn.com.

Consider these questions as you read:

1. Do you agree with the argument that because most gamers never become mass shooters, violent games are unlikely to be the cause of shootings? Explain your answer.
2. Do you think it is possible to release frustration and other negative feelings by playing nonviolent video games instead of violent ones? Explain your answer.
3. Taking into account the facts and arguments presented in this discussion, how persuasive is the argument that violent video games do not cause mass shootings? Which arguments provide the strongest support for this perspective, and why?

Editor's note: The discussion that follows presents common arguments made in support of this perspective, reinforced by facts, quotes, and examples taken from various sources.

Video games are a common form of entertainment around the world. In the United States the Entertainment Software Association estimates that 58 percent of Americans play video games. Estimates for youth are even higher. According to a recent report by the market research company NPD Group, 91 percent of youth ages two to seventeen play video games. Some of the most popular games are extremely violent. For instance, the *Huffington Post* describes the hugely popular *Call of Duty: Black Ops II* this way: "This gritty, extremely violent military first-person shooter involves constant killing using realistic weapons, with blood and gore pouring across the screen during more intense scenes."[50] Yet while large numbers of people play violent games like this, very few go on shooting rampages. Mass shootings are rare and unpredictable events, and researchers do not have a good understanding of what prompts a person to become a shooter. There is absolutely no evidence that violent video game play is the cause.

No Evidence Linking Games and Shootings

Although studies show that playing violent video games heightens aggression in some people, this is a far cry from proving a direct link between these games and mass shootings. Aggression is not always harmful or even threatening. Well-known video games researcher Christopher J. Ferguson says the level of aggression seen in many studies is "the equivalent of kids sticking their tongues out at each other."[51]

The problem with any of the studies that attempt to find a link between video game violence and real-world violence is that such studies are extremely limited. It is simply not ethical for researchers to conduct studies in which participants actually harm one another. Instead, they can only study things such as whether participants feel angry or would like to hurt another person. Brad Bushman, another prominent games researcher, says that as a result, it is impossible for researchers to understand whether video games make players more likely to commit a crime such as a shooting. "Are . . . [game players] more likely to stab someone? I dunno. Are they more likely to shoot somebody? I don't know. Are they more likely to rape someone? Beats me." He explains, "Those are very rare events and we can't study them ethically, so I don't know what the link is between playing violent video games and violent criminal behavior."[52]

A number of government reports and decisions have also confirmed the absence of a verifiable connection between violent game play and mass shootings. Following the 1999 Columbine shooting, the US Secret Service and the US Department of Education launched an investigation in an attempt to understand why shootings occur and how they might be prevented. They examined school shootings that occurred between

No Correlation Between Violent Game Play and Gun Violence

If violent video games caused mass shootings and other types of violent crime, then those countries where game play is most common should have the highest rates of gun-related deaths. Instead, as this graph shows, in most cases the countries with the highest rates of play (measured by video-game spending) actually have low rates of gun-related murder. The only exception is the United States, which has a high percentage of gamers and gun-related murders.

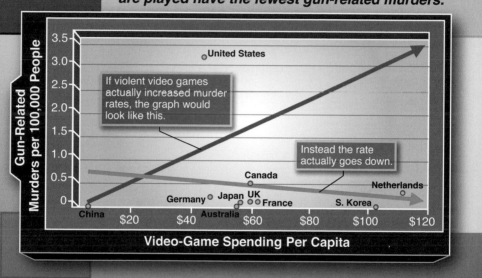

Violence and Guns

The nations where the most violent video games are played have the fewest gun-related murders.

If violent video games actually increased murder rates, the graph would look like this.

Instead the rate actually goes down.

Source: Stephen Marche, "Guns Are Beautiful: To Stop Gun Violence We Need to Stop Fetishizing Guns," *Esquire*, March 2013. www.esquire.com.

1974 and June 2000. Their analysis did not reveal video game violence as an important causal factor. In fact, they found that only 12 percent of the shooters had shown an interest in violent video games. In 2011 the US Supreme Court also weighed in on the matter. The court rejected a California ban on violent games for children, based in part on the opinion that there is no evidence that such games even cause children to act aggressively. Another report, this one released in 2013 by the CDC, states that there is no proven link between real-life firearm violence and violence in video games and other media. Investigations by the Australian and Swedish governments have reached similar conclusions.

Most Gamers Do Not Shoot People

The types of video games that frequently get the blame for mass shootings are extremely popular with youth and even many adults. That so many young people play these games should be seen as a clear indication of their harmless nature. The majority of people who play violent video games never commit mass shootings or any type of serious violence. As public health consultant Cheryl Olson says, "It's true that the Newtown, Conn., shooter apparently played violent video games. But the local kids on your soccer team, your 13-year-old boys who live down the street from you, they're all playing these violent games, too."[53]

Some of the countries with the highest numbers of video game players actually have very low rates of mass shootings. The *Washington Post* reports, "Looking at the world's 10 largest video game markets yields no evident, statistical correlation between video game consumption and gun-related killings. . . . In fact, countries where video game consumption is highest tend to be some of the safest countries in the world."[54] For example, gaming is extremely popular in Japan, yet shootings of any kind are extremely rare there. In 2008—the most recent statistics available—there were only eleven firearm-related homicides in Japan. This is one of the lowest rates in the world.

> "It's true that the Newtown, Conn., shooter apparently played violent video games. But the local kids on your soccer team, your 13-year-old boys who live down the street from you, they're all playing these violent games, too."[53]
>
> —Cheryl Olson is codirector of the Harvard Medical School Center for Mental Health and Media.

Games Prevent Violence

For some people, violent game play is actually a way to harmlessly release feelings of aggression, frustration, and boredom. Instead of letting out these feelings in the real world, where there is the potential for other people to be harmed, players can vent negative feelings in the virtual game world. Some people believe that the 1999 shooting at Columbine High School was the result of teenagers Dylan Klebold and Eric Harris losing this outlet for release. The teens were avid game players, and researcher and psychiatrist Jerald Block speculated that their rampage was not actually a result of violent game play, but because the shooters were cut off from it. After investigating the incident, he says that the Harris and Klebold used computer games as a way to express their rage, and when their parents denied them computer access, they had no way to vent their frustrations. He says, "Very soon thereafter—a couple of days—they started to plan the actual attack."[55]

> "Countries where video game consumption is highest tend to be some of the safest countries in the world."[54]
>
> —Max Fisher is a journalist who writes for the *Washington Post*.

Video game player Aaron Sampson talks about how school has caused him considerable stress and violent games have served as an important outlet for his frustrations. He says:

> My anger over school came to a head in college when I reached a breaking point somewhere in my sophomore year. . . . I was in an Asian studies class with a teacher who embodied everything I hated about bad teachers. He was giving us a test that involved pure and pointless memorization and regurgitation, and I decided to write him some notes, on the exam, about how useless the exam was.[56]

Sampson says he decided to flunk out of the class as a way to vent his feelings and take control of the situation. A year later, however, he says that another angry student at the same school shot and killed a teacher, and this event made him think about what prevented him from similar violent action. In his opinion, video games were a key factor. He says, "My time blowing off steam and relaxing with video games . . . played a part in diffusing that moment." He insists that giving people like him access to violent games is crucial to preventing violence, arguing, "When I hear Senators talking about violent video games and the media making false correlations between violent video games, firearms, and actual violence, I want to stop these people from making a huge mistake and eliminating one of the most calming factors of my life."[57]

Misguided Blame

Despite the lack of evidence, critics continue to blame violent video games for mass shootings. Ferguson argues that this insistence on connecting games and shootings stems from the human desire to understand these devastating events. For example, he talks about how society struggled to understand the 2012 Connecticut shooting, in which most of the victims were six- and seven-year-old children, and to prevent another shooting like that from ever occurring. He says, "If violent video games were some small but critical component of Lanza's motivation, why we could just get rid of such games and make this whole problem go away." However, such thoughts are misguided. Ferguson adds, "It's a tempting belief but absolutely wrong."[58] The fact is that there is no evidence that video game violence causes mass shootings.

Chapter Four

Would Improvements in Mental Health Care Reduce Mass Shootings?

Improvements in Mental Health Care Would Reduce Mass Shootings

- There is evidence that mental illness is a factor in many mass shootings.
- Too many people who are mentally ill do not receive treatment.
- Treatment can reduce the risk of violent behavior in people with mental illness.
- Restricting the ability of the mentally ill to purchase guns would help reduce shootings.

The Debate at a Glance

Improvements in Mental Health Care Would Not Reduce Mass Shootings

- There is no scientific evidence that mental illness causes mass shootings.
- Most people with mental illness never act violently, let alone become mass shooters.
- It is virtually impossible to predict who is likely to become a mass shooter.
- Focusing on mental illness might actually increase the risk of shootings by deterring people from seeking treatment.

Improvements in Mental Health Care Would Reduce Mass Shootings

"Strengthening gun control won't stop the next mass shooter, but changing our attitudes, the treatment options we offer and the laws for holding the mentally unstable and mentally ill for treatment just might."

—Mel Robbins is a legal analyst.

Mel Robbins, "The Real Gun Problem Is Mental Health, Not the IRA," CNN, June 25, 2014. www.cnn.com.

Consider these questions as you read:

1. Do you agree with the argument that inadequate treatment of the mentally ill puts society at risk for mass shootings? Explain.
2. How strong is the argument that psychiatric medications contribute to shootings? Explain your answer.
3. Do you think it would be possible to ensure that the mentally ill are unable to purchase a gun in United States? Why or why not?

Editor's note: The discussion that follows presents common arguments made in support of this perspective, reinforced by facts, quotes, and examples taken from various sources.

In May 2014 twenty-two-year-old Elliot Rodger went on a killing spree near the University of California campus in Santa Barbara. Starting with his roommates, he shot and stabbed multiple victims, killing six people and wounding thirteen before he killed himself. After the incident, investigations revealed that there had been warning signs prior to Rodger's violent behavior. According to news reports, he had a history of mental health problems and had been seeing therapists on a regular basis since he was young. In fact, in the month before the shooting, his family had contacted the police after they discovered YouTube posts in which he talked about suicide and killing people. Police even came to his house to investigate but left after Rodger convinced them that it was a misunderstanding and that he had no intention of hurting anyone. After police left, Rodger continued his preparations. In a manifesto he left behind, he talks about why he was planning this "day of retribution." He says, "All of those beautiful girls I've desired so much in my life, but can never have because they despise and loathe me, I will destroy. All of those popular people who live hedonistic lives of pleasure, I will destroy, because they never accepted me as one of them. I will kill them all and make them suffer, just as they have made me suffer. It is only fair."[59]

Clearly, Rodger was a disturbed individual. Although no one can be absolutely certain, it is highly likely that a more advanced and well-funded mental health system could have prevented this tragedy. It is vitally important for the United States to improve the mental health system. New York lawyer Carolyn Reinach Wolf, who works with people struggling with mental illness, says, "We need to have a discussion about people with mental health issues and how we get them into treatment to lead more normal lives. In turn, I believe, there will be less acting out, less violence." Referring to the 2012 Sandy Hook school shooting, she adds, "Think about it: someone who is mentally stable doesn't walk into an elementary school and shoot little children between the eyes. It just doesn't happen."[60]

> "Think about it: someone who is mentally stable doesn't walk into an elementary school and shoot little children between the eyes. It just doesn't happen."[60]
>
> —Carolyn Reinach Wolf is a lawyer who works with people struggling with mental illness.

Lack of Treatment

Research shows that mental illness is a significant factor in many mass shootings, so improving mental health care is crucial to preventing such shootings. News publication *Mother Jones* has extensively researched US mass shootings. According to its analysis of shootings in the past thirty years, in about two-thirds of cases the shooter exhibited prior signs of

Mental Illness Is a Common Factor in Mass Shootings

Research by Stanford University supports the view that improvements in mental health care would reduce mass shootings. Statistics on mass shootings that have occurred in the United States between 1966 and 2013 reveal that the most common motivating factor in such shootings was mental illness. The data also shows that more people died in incidents involving mentally ill shooters than in shootings motivated by other factors. By improving mental health care, the United States could reduce mass shootings and the number of people harmed by these crimes.

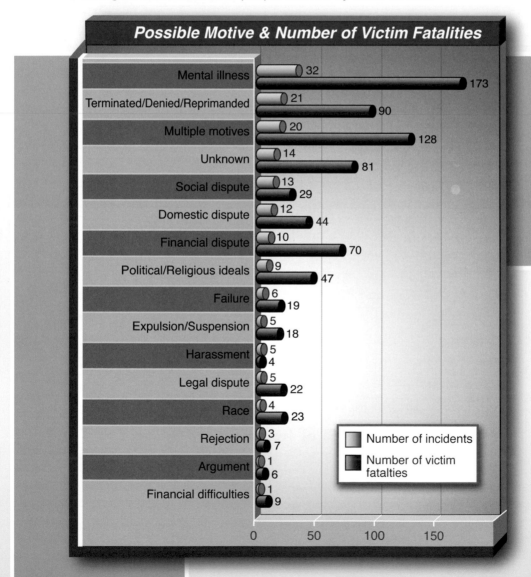

Possible Motive & Number of Victim Fatalities

Motive	Number of incidents	Number of victim fatalities
Mental illness	32	173
Terminated/Denied/Reprimanded	21	90
Multiple motives	20	128
Unknown	14	81
Social dispute	13	29
Domestic dispute	12	44
Financial dispute	10	70
Political/Religious ideals	9	47
Failure	6	19
Expulsion/Suspension	5	18
Harassment	5	4
Legal dispute	5	22
Race	4	23
Rejection	3	7
Argument	1	6
Financial difficulties	1	9

Source: Stanford University Libraries, "Geospatial Center Tracks Mass Shootings," Mass Shootings in America project, Stanford University, 2013. http://library.stanford.edu.

mental illness. Another study, the Mass Shootings in America project by Stanford University Libraries, found that more than half of mass shooting incidents since 1996 were committed by people who suffered from some sort of mental illness. Stanford's research also shows that mass shooters who are mentally ill often inflict more casualties than mass shooters who do not have a history of mental illness. Since 1996, according to this research, mass shootings committed by people with mental illness resulted in 1,054 dead and wounded compared to 581 deaths and injuries in cases involving a shooter who had no history of mental illness. Although mental illness does not automatically lead to violent acts, these statistics demonstrate that mental illness remains a factor in a significant number of mass shootings.

Unfortunately, in the United States too many mentally ill individuals are never identified or treated. According to the Substance Abuse and Mental Health Services Administration (SAMHSA), in 2011 an estimated 45.6 million adults aged eighteen or older in the United States had suffered some type of mental illness in the past year. This is almost 20 percent of the adult population. Within that group only about 38 percent had received mental health services in the past year. The percentage of those with a severe mental illness—such as bipolar disorder or schizophrenia—who received treatment was higher, however even among this group, less than 60 percent received treatment.

The most common reason reported for this lack of treatment was that patients could not afford it. Mental health care can be expensive, and according to a 2013 *Newsweek* report, nearly half of private psychiatrists do not accept health insurance or Medicare. Other common reasons were the belief that treatment was not necessary, not having time for treatment, or not knowing where to go to get it. Tara F. Bishop, an assistant professor of public health and medicine at Weill Cornell Medical College, has researched the topic and warns that this lack of treatment is dangerous. She says, "We're putting people in unsafe situations."[61]

Treatment Reduces Violence

There is evidence that when people receive care for mental health issues, they are far less likely to engage in violent behavior of any sort. In a 2014 article in the *Lancet*, researchers report the results of a study of more than eighty thousand people who were prescribed antipsychotic or mood-stabilizing medication in Sweden between 2006 and 2009. The researchers found that violent crime among this population decreased significantly while they were taking this medication. As Robert N. Davison, executive director of the Mental Health Association of Essex County, New Jersey, says, "Study after study has shown that treatment reduces the incidence of violence among those with severe mental illness."[62]

Communication Is Lacking

However, even if improvements in care and treatment were made, there remains a huge gap in terms of communication between agencies. A well-functioning mental health system would communicate regularly with other government agencies to ensure that people with mental illness cannot buy guns. There are too many cases where mass shooters have exhibited mental problems and have even been seeing mental health professionals yet were legally allowed to purchase the weapons they later used in a shooting. For example, journalist Mark Follman discusses the 2011 shooting by Jared Loughner, who killed six people and wounded thirteen at a shopping center in Arizona. Follman says, "For several years prior, Loughner had displayed signs of serious mental illness, including outbursts during his high school classes and complaints about voices in his head. Nevertheless, he was able to stroll into a Sportsmen's Warehouse in Tucson and purchase a weapon and ammunition legally."[63] Loughner is not the only shooter who has shown signs of mental illness but still been able to legally purchase a gun. Of the sixty-two mass shootings analyzed by Follman and other journalists who conducted this investigation for news publication *Mother Jones*, 80 percent of the shooters obtained their weapons legally,

> "At the heart of the problem is the sheer number of people being failed by our nation's mental illness treatment system and left untreated."[64]
>
> —E. Fuller Torrey, founder of the Treatment Advocacy Center, an organization that works to increase treatment of mental illness.

but a large number had shown signs of mental health problems.

There is widespread evidence that untreated mental illness plays a role in a significant number of mass shootings. E. Fuller Torrey, founder of the Treatment Advocacy Center, which works to increase treatment of mental illness, argues that many mass shootings and other crimes can be prevented through more effective treatment. He says, "At the heart of the problem is the sheer number of people being failed by our nation's mental illness treatment system and left untreated." However, he insists, "This is preventable."[64] The United States needs to significantly improve its mental health care system. By improving the identification and treatment of individuals at risk for violence, and by making sure they do not have easy access to weapons, the United States can reduce mass shootings.

Improvements in Mental Health Care Would Not Reduce Mass Shootings

"Providing effective, widely available mental health care is important and can benefit individuals with mental health issues, their families and society at large. But thinking it will make a dent in mass shootings is not borne out by the evidence."

—Mark Robison is a journalist for the *Reno Gazette-Journal.*

Mark Robison, "Will Better Mental Health Care Decrease Mass Shootings?," *RGJ.com*, April 21, 2013. http://blogs.rgj.com.

Consider these questions as you read:

1. Do you agree with the argument that it is rare for the mentally ill to be violent? Why or why not?
2. How strong is the argument that there is no scientific evidence linking mental illness with mass shootings? Explain.
3. How persuasive is the argument that improvements in mental health care will not prevent mass shootings? Which arguments are strongest?

Editor's note: The discussion that follows presents common arguments made in support of this perspective, reinforced by facts, quotes, and examples taken from various sources.

Elliot Rodger, the young man who killed six people in Santa Barbara in 2014, had a history of mental health problems. Predictably, that attack sparked a wave of blame and introspection over the state of mental health care in America. Politicians and others immediately called for more attention to be given to the problems of mental illness. Many insist that the government should have greater authority to restrict the freedom of people with mental illness in order to reduce the risk of them harming others. For example, journalist Rachel Alexander points out that this was what happened in the past. She says, "Up until the 1960s, the severely mentally ill were locked up in psychiatric hospitals, for their own good and for the protection of society." She argues that the United States should revert to a similar system. "This isn't going to be popular to say, but the laws must be changed to make it easier to lock people up—even against their will."[65]

This position flies in the face of reality. The fact is, people with mental illness rarely commit mass shootings—or any other publicly violent acts. The idea of incarcerating these people without strong proof that they pose a real risk to society is an absolute violation of their rights. The editorial board of *USA Today* explains how US laws have changed to respect these rights. It says:

> Until the 1970s, snatching people with symptoms off the street and committing them to an institution was permissible. So was keeping them there, no matter their mental state. But a string of court decisions changed the rules by recognizing that the mentally ill have civil rights, and by requiring strong evidence of imminent danger to themselves or others before they can be committed against their will.[66]

Such strong evidence rarely exists in connection with mass shootings, either before or after. In fact, while mental illness often receives intense media attention in relation to mass shootings, research shows that numerous other factors appear to have a far stronger correlation with these tragic events. Although America's mental health system can always be improved, the intense focus on mental illness in the wake of such shootings is misguided and will not help prevent more mass shootings.

No Scientific Evidence

The problem with linking mental illness to mass shootings is that this link is not supported by scientific evidence. The absence of evidence is not for lack of trying. Numerous researchers have analyzed past incidents

Mental Illness Is Not a Significant Factor in Mass Shootings

Mental illness is often cited as a primary cause of mass shootings, but research suggests otherwise. An analysis of mass shootings that took place between January 2009 and July 2014 found little documented evidence of mental health issues in most of the shooters. In only 11 percent of the shootings was there any evidence that concerns about the shooter's mental health had been brought to the attention of a medical professional, a legal authority, or a school official before the shooting.

Mental Health Concerns

11%

Source: Mayors Against Illegal Guns, "Analysis of Recent Mass Shootings," Everytown for Gun Safety, July 17, 2014. www.everytown.org.

in an effort to understand what makes a person commit such a terrible and public crime. Thus far, there is no strong evidence that mental illness is a major factor. For example, Everytown for Gun Safety, a movement working to end gun violence, analyzed mass shootings that occurred between January 2009 and July 2014. Concerns about the mental health of the shooter had been brought to the attention of a legal authority, doctor, or school official in only 11 percent of those cases. A large study on mass murderers was reported in the *Journal of the American Academy of Child and Adolescent Psychiatry* in 2001. Researchers analyzed American youth age nineteen or younger who had killed three or more victims between 1958 and 1999. They concluded that although it is virtually impossible to predict a mass shooting or other type of mass murder, there are some characteristics that the perpetrators have in common. The researchers found that 70 percent of the killers were described as loners, 62 percent had problems with substance abuse, 48 percent had a preoccupation with war or weapons, 43 percent had been victims of bullying, and 42 percent had a history of violence. Only 23 percent had any type of documented psychiatric history. This means that the majority of killers—about three-quarters—did not have a documented history of mental illness.

While it is true that some mass shooters suffer from mental illness, there is no proof that their illness was the cause of the shootings. Paolo del Vecchio is director of SAMHSA's Center for Mental Health Services. When consulted for a 2013 article in the *Reno Gazette-Journal*, he reported that he is unaware of any peer-reviewed studies showing a relationship between mental illness and mass murder. In fact, most people with mental illness never commit any violent crimes, let alone mass shootings. Researchers estimate that only about 4 percent of all violent crimes in the United States are perpetrated by people who are mentally ill. *New York Times* correspondent Margot Sanger-Katz explains the implications of this. She says,

> "Can we reliably predict violence? 'No' is the short answer."[68]
>
> — Jeffrey Swanson is a professor of psychiatry at Duke University and an expert in the causes of violence.

"If mental illness could be eliminated as a factor in violent crime, the overall rate would be reduced by only 4 percent. That means 96 percent of violent crimes . . . are committed by people without any mental-health problems at all." As a result, she argues, "Solutions that focus on reducing crimes by the mentally ill will make only a small dent in the nation's rate of gun-related murders, ranging from mass killings to shootings that claim a single victim."[67]

A Dangerous Expectation

Suggesting that improvements in mental health will help identify and stop potential mass shooters creates dangerously false expectations that this will make society safe from shootings. In fact, it is almost impossible to identify in advance who will become a mass shooter. Jeffrey Swanson is a professor of psychiatry at Duke University and an expert in the causes of violence. He says, "Can we reliably predict violence? 'No' is the short answer. Psychiatrists, using clinical judgment, are not much better than chance at predicting which individual patients will do something violent and which will not."[68]

John Monahan is a professor at the University of Virginia whose work has focused on the science of violence prediction. Based on his research, he agrees that the ability of mental health professionals to predict who will commit a violent act is only slightly better than chance. Further, he says that these studies on violence have been about more common types of violence, such as hitting another person. He says, "To predict something as rare as a mass shooting is like trying to find a very small needle in a very large haystack."[69]

> "To predict something as rare as a mass shooting is like trying to find a very small needle in a very large haystack."[69]
>
> —John Monahan is a professor at the University of Virginia whose work has focused on the science of violence prediction.

Focusing on the Mentally Ill Is Not the Answer

Not only is an increased focus on mental health care unlikely to reduce mass shootings, it may actually reduce the number of people who seek treatment. This would exacerbate the problem. Critics insist that people suffering from mental illness need to be identified and treated, prevented from owning guns, and monitored in case they show signs of violence. However, Richard A. Friedman, a professor of clinical psychiatry and the director of the psychopharmacology clinic at the Weill Cornell Medical College, explains that such aggressive actions could be problematic. He says, "In the wake of these horrific killings, it would be understandable if the public wanted to make it easier to force treatment on patients before a threat is issued. But that might simply discourage other mentally ill people from being candid and drive some of the sickest patients away from the mental health care system."[70] As a result, the threat of violence from the mentally ill would actually increase.

Because some mass shooters have also been mentally ill, it is natural to look to improving the mental health system as a way of preventing future shootings. However, the reality is that the risk posed by the mentally ill is actually very small, and any improvements to the mental health system are unlikely to reduce that number significantly. As Friedman says, "We have always had—and always will have—Adam Lanzas and Elliot Rodgers. The sobering fact is that there is little we can do to predict or change human behavior, particularly violence."[71]

Source Notes

Overview: Mass Shootings

1. Quoted in Casey Wian, Jim Spellman, and Michael Pearson, "'He Intended to Kill Them All,' Prosecutor in Theater Shooting Says," CNN, January 9, 2013. www.cnn.com.
2. Mark Follman, "What Exactly Is a Mass Shooting?," *Mother Jones*, August 24, 2012. www.motherjones.com.
3. Jerome P. Bjelopera et al. "Public Mass Shootings in the United States: Selected Implications for Federal Public Health and Safety Policy," Congressional Research Service, March 18, 2013. http://fas.org.
4. J. Pete Blair and Katherine W. Schweit, "A Study of Active Shooter Incidents, 2000–2013," Texas State University and Federal Bureau of Investigation, US Department of Justice, 2014. www.fbi.gov.
5. Barack Obama, "Remarks by the President at the Memorial Service for Victims of the Navy Yard Shooting," White House, September 22, 2013. www.whitehouse.gov.

Chapter One: Are Mass Shootings a Serious Problem?

6. Quoted in Alan Duke, "Loughner Sentenced to Life for Arizona Shootings," CNN, November 8, 2012. www.cnn.com.
7. Quoted in Duke, "Loughner Sentenced to Life for Arizona Shootings."
8. Blair and Schweit, "A Study of Active Shooter Incidents, 2000–2013."
9. Eric Holder, "Attorney General Eric Holder Delivers Remarks at the International Association of Chiefs of Police Annual Conference," US Department of Justice, October 21, 2013. www.justice.gov.
10. Quoted in Josh Sanburn, "Why the FBI Report That Mass Shootings Are Up Can Be Misleading," *Time*, September 26, 2014. http://time.com.
11. *USA Today*, "Behind the Bloodshed: The Untold Story of America's Mass Killings," 2013. www.usatoday.com.
12. Blair and Schweit, "A Study of Active Shooter Incidents, 2000–2013."

13. White House, "Now Is the Time: The President's Plan to Protect Our Children and Our Communities by Reducing Gun Violence," January 16, 2013. www.whitehouse.gov.
14. Josh Blackman, "Is There Really an Epidemic of Mass Shootings?," *American Spectator*, June 9, 2014. http://spectator.org.
15. Laura Smith-Spark, "Are Mass Killings on the Increase? Criminologist Says No," CNN, April 3, 2013. www.cnn.com.
16. Jesse Walker, "Why Can't Anyone Agree How Many Mass Shootings There Have Been in 2013?," *Reason*, September 19, 2013. http://reason.com.
17. Quoted in Sanburn, "Why the FBI Report That Mass Shootings Are Up Can Be Misleading."
18. Quoted in John Tedesco, "Mass Shootings Horrifying but Statistically Rare," *San Antonio (TX) Express-News*, July 20, 2012. www.mysanantonio.com.
19. Quoted in Associated Press, "Mass Shootings Are Not Growing in Frequency, Experts Say," *Daily News*, December 15, 2012. www.nydailynews.com.
20. Quoted in *Kottke.org* (blog), "Roger Ebert on the Media's Coverage of School Shootings," December 14, 2012. http://kottke.org.
21. Quoted in Scott Neuman, "Violence in Schools: How Big a Problem Is It?," NPR, March 16, 2012. www.npr.org.
22. Quoted in Neuman, "Violence in Schools."
23. Quoted in Tedesco, "Mass Shootings Horrifying but Statistically Rare."

Chapter Two: Will Stricter Gun Control Reduce Mass Shootings?

24. Quoted in Fawn Johnson, "Why Gun Control Can't Eliminate Gun Violence," *National Journal*, September 18, 2013. www.nationaljournal.com.
25. Colin Goddard, comment on *New York Times Upfront*, "Is It Too Easy to Get a Gun?," November 19, 2012. http://upfront.scholastic.com.
26. Quoted in Mark Follman and Gavin Aronsen, "'A Killing Machine': Half of All Mass Shooters Used High-Capacity Magazines," *Mother Jones*, January 30, 2013. www.motherjones.com.

27. Quoted in Susan Candiotti and Dana Ford, "Connecticut School Victims Were Shot Multiple Times," CNN, December 15, 2012. www.cnn.com.

28. *Economist*, "Newtown's Horror; Gun Violence in America," December 22, 2012. www.economist.com.

29. James Stern, "'Point . . . Counterpoint,' in 'Special Report: Violence & Entertainment,'" *Variety*, vol. 429, no. 10. http://variety.com.

30. Mark Follman, "The NRA Myth of Arming the Good Guys," *Mother Jones*, December 28, 2012. www.motherjones.com.

31. Wayne LaPierre, "NRA Press Conference," National Rifle Association, December 21, 2012. http://home.nra.org.

32. LaPierre, "NRA Press Conference."

33. Quoted in Jeffrey Goldberg, "The Case for More Guns (and More Gun Control): How Do We Reduce Gun Crime and Aurora-Style Mass Shootings When Americans Already Own Nearly 300 Million Guns?," *Atlantic*, December 2012. www.theatlantic.com.

34. Mike Hammond, "'Point . . . Counterpoint,' in 'Special Report: Violence & Entertainment,'" *Variety*, vol. 429, no. 10. http://variety.com.

35. James Alan Fox, "Gun Control or Carry Permits Won't Stop Mass Murder," CNN, July 21, 2012. www.cnn.com.

36. *McDonald v. Chicago*, 561 US ___, 2010.

37. Kevin D. Williamson, "Armed, Not Dangerous: Every Swiss Man Is Trained to Shoot, So Why Don't They?," *National Review*, February 11, 2013. www.nationalreview.com.

38. Thomas Sowell, "Gun-Control Ignorance," *National Review*, December 18, 2012. www.nationalreview.com.

39. Quoted in Garrett Haake, "Romney on NBC: Changing Gun Laws Won't 'Make All Bad Things Go Away,'" NBC News, January 15, 2013. www.nbcnews.com.

Chapter Three: Do Violent Video Games Cause Mass Shootings?

40. Quoted in David Blair, "Anders Behring Breivik's Norway Shooting Spree Relived in Chilling Detail," *Telegraph* (London), October 20, 2012. www.telegraph.co.uk.

41. Quoted in D.G. Singer and J.L. Singer, eds., *Handbook of Children and the Media*, 2nd ed. Thousand Oaks, CA: Sage, 2012, p. 257.

42. Media Violence Commission, "Report of the Media Violence Commission," *Aggressive Behavior*, 2012. www.israsociety.com.

43. Brad Bushman, interviewed by Jeffrey Brown, "Can Violent Video Games Play a Role in Violent Behavior?," PBS, February 19, 2013. www.pbs.org.

44. Quoted in Jane E. Allen, "Psych Experts: Violent Videos Distort Kids' Health, Perceptions," ABC News, June 28, 2011. http://abc news.go.com.

45. Brad Bushman, "Do Violent Games Play a Role in Shootings?," CNN, September 18, 2013. www.cnn.com.

46. Quoted in Tia Ghose, "Mass Shooting Psychology: Spree Killers Have Consistent Profile, Research Shows," *Huffington Post*, December 19, 2012. www.huffingtonpost.com.

47. Nancy Gibbs and Timothy Roche, "The Columbine Tapes," *Time*, December 20, 1999. http://content.time.com.

48. Quoted in Gibbs and Roche, "The Columbine Tapes."

49. Bushman, "Do Violent Games Play a Role in Shootings?"

50. Jinny Gudmundsen, "10 Most Violent Video Games (and 10+ Alternatives)," *Huffington Post*, June 24, 2013. www.huffingtonpost.com.

51. Quoted in Kathryn Doyle, "Violent Video Games May Be Tied to Aggressive Thoughts," Reuters, March 24, 2014. http://uk.reuters.com.

52. Quoted in Jason Schreier, "From Halo to Hot Sauce: What 25 Years of Violent Video Game Research Looks Like," *Kotaku* (blog), January 17, 2013. http://kotaku.com.

53. Jeffrey Brown, "Can Violent Video Games Play a Role in Violent Behavior?"

54. Max Fisher, "Ten-Country Comparison Suggests There's Little or No Link Between Video Games and Gun Murders," *Washington Post*, December 17, 2012. www.washingtonpost.com.

55. Quoted in Katy Human, "Study Links Computer Denial to Columbine," *Denver Post*, July 5, 2007. www.denverpost.com.

56. Aaron Sampson, "In Defense of Video Game Violence: A Personal Account of the Impact of Gaming, Gun Ownership, and Growing Up," *Gamespot*, February 7, 2013. www.gamespot.com.

57. Sampson, "In Defense of Video Game Violence."

58. Christopher J. Ferguson, "Video Games Didn't Cause Newtown Rampage," CNN, February 20, 2013. www.cnn.com.

Chapter Four: Would Improvements in Mental Health Care Reduce Mass Shootings?

59. Elliot Rodger, "My Twisted World: The Story of Elliot Rodger," *New York Times*, May 25, 2014. www.nytimes.com.
60. Quoted in Jennifer Bendery, "Suicide Is Leading Cause of Gun Deaths, but Largely Absent in Debate on Gun Violence," *Huffington Post*, May 14, 2013. www.huffingtonpost.com.
61. Quoted in Victoria Bekiempis, "This Lack of Psychiatric Care Is Madness," *Newsweek*, December 13, 2013. www.newsweek.com.
62. Robert N. Davison, "Re 'When Right to Bear Arms Includes the Mentally Ill,'" letter to the editor, *New York Times*, December 25, 2013. www.nytimes.com.
63. Mark Follman, "Mass Shootings: Maybe What We Need Is a Better Mental-Health Policy," *Mother Jones*, November 9, 2012. www.motherjones.com.
64. Quoted in Treatment Advocacy Center, "Role of Untreated Severe Mental Illness Missing from New FBI Report," September 26, 2014. www.treatmentadvocacycenter.org.
65. Rachel Alexander, "Mass Shootings: It's Time to Go Back to Institutionalizing the Severely Mentally Ill," Townhall, June 23, 2014. http://townhall.com.
66. Editorial Board, "Should 11 Million Mentally Ill Be Locked Up? Our View," *USA Today*, September 26, 2013. www.usatoday.com.
67. Margot Sanger-Katz, "Why Improving Mental Health Would Do Little to End Gun Violence," *National Journal*, January 24, 2013. www.nationaljournal.com.
68. Quoted in Richard A. Friedman, "In Gun Debate, a Misguided Focus on Mental Illness," *New York Times*, December 17, 2012. www.nytimes.com.
69. Quoted in Sanger-Katz, "Why Improving Mental Health Would Do Little to End Gun Violence."
70. Richard A. Friedman, "Why Can't Doctors Identify Killers?," *New York Times*, May 27, 2014. www.nytimes.com.
71. Friedman, "Why Can't Doctors Identify Killers?"

Mass Shootings Facts

The Threat of Mass Shootings

- A *USA Today* analysis of mass killings between 2007 and 2013 shows that in that time, 934 people died in mass killings, most of which were shootings.
- Everytown for Gun Safety estimates that in 2012 fewer than 1 percent of gun murder victims in the United States were killed in mass shootings.
- According to the Mass Shootings in America project by Stanford University Libraries, an analysis of the data since 1996 shows that California ranks highest for the number of shooting incidents, the number of victims injured, and the number of people killed.
- *Mother Jones* reports that of the seventy mass shootings that have occurred in the United States since 1982, seven took place in 2012.
- According to a 2012 report in the *Washington Times*, fifteen of the twenty-five worst mass shootings in the past fifty years happened in the United States.
- The Congressional Research Service reports that US mass shootings between 1983 and 2012 resulted in 1,023 total deaths and injuries, not including the deaths of shooters.

Gun Laws

- According to the Small Arms Survey, in the United States there are approximately 270 million guns, or 88.9 per 100 people.
- In a December 2012 poll of 1,038 adult Americans, Gallup found that 44 percent of people are in favor of a ban on semiautomatic guns, also known as assault rifles.
- Everytown for Gun Safety analyzed mass shootings between January 2009 and July 2014 in which at least four people were murdered with a gun and found that only 14 percent of the shootings took place in public spaces where it was not lawful to carry a gun.

- The organization Mayors Against Illegal Guns analyzed fifty-six mass shootings that occurred between January 2009 and January 2013. It found that at least thirteen involved assault weapons or high-capacity magazines.
- A 2012 poll of 1,922 Americans conducted for Thomson Reuters found that 91 percent of people support background checks for gun purchasers.

Violent Video Games and Mass Shootings

- The Entertainment Software Association reports there is no link between video games and violent crime such as shootings; it says that although video game sales more than tripled between 1998 and 2012, violent crime decreased dramatically.
- In a study published in the *Journal of Experimental Social Psychology* in 2011, researchers report that in a study of seventy young adults, those who played violent games for twenty-five minutes had a smaller brain response when exposed to violent images than those who played nonviolent games.
- In a 2012 poll of 1,009 adults, Gallup found that 47 percent believe that decreasing the depiction of gun violence on television, in movies, and in video games would be a very effective approach to preventing mass shootings.
- The Entertainment Software Association reports that in 2011, 18.4 percent of the games sold were shooter games.

Mental Illness

- According to a 2012 Gallup poll of 1,009 adults, 50 percent of those surveyed believe that increased government spending on mental health screening and treatment would be a very effective way to prevent mass shootings at schools.
- SAMHSA reports that among the 4.9 million adults who did not receive needed mental health care in 2011, approximately 16 percent said they did not know where to go for care, and about 15 percent said they did not have time for care.

- The National Institute of Mental Health's Epidemiologic Catchment Area study, one of the largest studies to examine mental illness and rates of treatment in the United States, showed that violence was reported in about 2 percent of people with no psychiatric disorder and in about 8 percent of people with schizophrenia.
- According to the National Alliance on Mental Illness, one in seventeen Americans lives with a serious mental illness such as schizophrenia, major depression, or bipolar disorder.
- Everytown for Gun Safety reports that of the 110 mass shootings that occurred in the United States between January 2009 and July 2014, in only 12 cases was there evidence that concerns about the mental health of the shooter had been brought to the attention of a medical, school, or legal authority.

Related Organizations and Websites

Brady Center to Prevent Gun Violence
1225 Eye St. NW, Suite 1100
Washington, DC 20005
phone: (202) 898-0792 • fax: (202) 371-9615
website: www.bradynetwork.org

The Brady Center aims to reduce mass shootings and other types of gun violence in the United States. It works to enact and enforce regulations and public policies that will increase public awareness and reduce gun violence. Its website includes various facts, studies and reports, and information on current and proposed legislation.

Coalition to Stop Gun Violence
1424 L St. NW, Suite 2-1
Washington, DC 20005
phone: (202) 506-3985
e-mail: csgv@csgv.org • website: www.csgv.org

The Coalition to Stop Gun Violence seeks to reduce gun violence through research and effective policy advocacy. Its coalition members include religious organizations, child welfare advocates, public health professionals, and social justice organizations. Its website has information about various issues related to gun control.

Entertainment Software Association
575 Seventh St. NW, Suite 300
Washington, DC 20004
website: www.theesa.com

The Entertainment Software Association is the trade association for the US computer and video game industry. Its website contains numerous research reports, facts, and articles about video games.

Gun Owners of America
8001 Forbes Pl., Suite 102
Springfield, VA 22151
phone: (703) 321-8585 • fax: (703) 321-8408
website: www.gunowners.org

Gun Owners of America is a nonprofit lobbying organization formed in 1975 to preserve and defend the Second Amendment rights of gun owners. It believes firearms ownership is an important freedom of Americans and represents gun owners when their rights are threatened.

Law Center to Prevent Gun Violence
268 Bush St., #555
San Francisco, CA 94104
phone: (415) 433-2062 • fax: (415) 433-3357
website: http://smartgunlaws.org

The Law Center to Prevent Gun Violence is a nonprofit organization that is dedicated to preventing death caused by guns. Its website provides information about America's gun control laws.

Mayors Against Illegal Guns
website: www.mayorsagainstillegalguns.org

Mayors Against Illegal Guns is a coalition of more than 850 mayors from cities across the country. It works to share information and develop policies and laws that will help law enforcement target illegal guns. Its website has information about mass shootings and illegal use of guns in the United States, as well as reports and editorials about shootings.

National Institute of Mental Health (NIMH)
6001 Executive Blvd.
Rockville, MD 20852
phone: (866) 615-6464
website: www.nimh.nih.gov • e-mail: nimhinfo@mail.nik.gov

The NIMH is a government organization that works to increase understanding and treatment of mental illness. Its website includes information and statistics about mental illness in the United States.

National Rifle Association of America (NRA)
11250 Waples Mill Rd.
Fairfax, VA 22030
phone: (800) 672-3888
website: www.nra.org

The NRA was founded in 1871 and believes that Americans have a constitutional right to own firearms. It promotes gun safety through training and education.

Second Amendment Foundation
12500 NE Tenth Pl.
Bellevue, WA 98005
phone: (425) 454-7012 • fax: (425) 451-3959
website: www.saf.org

The Second Amendment Foundation believes Americans have a constitutional right to own firearms. It argues that this right should be granted to all citizens except violent criminals. The organization works to inform the public about the consequences of gun control.

Violence Policy Center
1730 Rhode Island Ave. NW, Suite 1014
Washington, DC 20036
phone: (202) 822-8200
website: www.vpc.org

The Violence Policy Center is a nonprofit organization that works to stop gun-related death and injury through research, advocacy, education, and collaboration. It believes that firearms should be subject to health and safety regulations, just like other consumer products are. Its website has information about firearms laws and numerous reports about gun-related violence and death.

For Further Research

Books

Glenn Beck, *Exposing the Truth About Guns*. New York: Threshold Editions, 2013.

Matt Doeden, *Gun Control: Preventing Violence or Crushing Constitutional Rights?* Minneapolis, MN: Twenty-First Century, 2012.

Brian Kevin, *Gun Rights & Responsibilities*. Minncapolis, MN: Abdo, 2012.

Steven J. Kirsh, *Children, Adolescents, and Media Violence: A Critical Look at the Research*. Los Angeles: Sage, 2012.

Robert Spitzer, *The Politics of Gun Control*, 5th ed. Boulder, CO: Paradigm, 2011.

Periodicals

Max Fisher, "Ten-Country Comparison Suggests There's Little or No Link Between Video Games and Gun Murders," *Washington Post*, December 17, 2012.

James Alan Fox, "Expert: 'Banning Violent Video Games Would Do Little to Avert the Next Mass Murder,'" *New York Daily News*, March 24, 2013.

Jeffrey Goldberg, "The Case for More Guns (and More Gun Control): How Do We Reduce Gun Crime and Aurora-Style Mass Shootings When Americans Already Own Nearly 300 Million Guns?," *Atlantic*, December 2012.

Margot Sanger-Katz, "Why Improving Mental Health Would Do Little to End Gun Violence," *National Journal*, January 24, 2013.

Internet Sources

Jerome P. Bjelopera et al. "Public Mass Shootings in the United States: Selected Implications for Federal Public Health and Safety Policy," Congressional Research Service, March 18, 2013. http://fas.org/sgp/crs/misc/R43004.pdf.

J. Pete Blair and Katherine W. Schweit, "A Study of Active Shooter Incidents, 2000–2013," Texas State University and Federal Bureau of Investigation, US Department of Justice, 2014. www.fbi.gov/news/stories/2014/september/fbi-releases-study-on-active-shooter-incidents/pdfs/a-study-of-active-shooter-incidents-in-the-u.s.-between-2000-and-2013.

Entertainment Software Association, "Essential Facts About Games and Violence," 2011. www.theesa.com/facts/pdfs/ESA_EF_About_Games_and_Violence.pdf.

Everytown for Gun Safety, "Analysis of Recent Mass Shootings," July 2014. https://s3.amazonaws.com/s3.everytown.org/images/MassShooting_v7_CS6_WEB.pdf.

Mark Follman, Gavin Aronson, Deanna Pan, and Maggie Caldwell, "A Guide to Mass Shootings in America," *Mother Jones*, May 24, 2013. www.motherjones.com/politics/2012/07/mass-shootings-map.

Mayors Against Illegal Guns, "Analysis of Recent Mass Shootings," 2013. http://libcloud.s3.amazonaws.com/9/56/4/1242/analysis-of-recent-mass-shootings.pdf.

White House, "Now Is the Time: The President's Plan to Protect Our Children and Our Communities by Reducing Gun Violence," January 16, 2013. www.whitehouse.gov/sites/default/files/docs/wh_now_is_the_time_full.pdf.

Index

Note: Boldface page numbers indicate illustrations.

About the Author

Andrea C. Nakaya, a native of New Zealand, holds a BA in English and an MA in communications from San Diego State University. She has written and edited more than thirty-five books on current issues. She currently lives in Encinitas, California, with her husband and their two children, Natalie and Shane.